A Creative Journey
Seth Inspired

Richard Kendall

Other books by Richard Kendall:
THE ROAD TO ELMIRA

Book and cover design, typography and cover photo by Deb Tejada of
TejadaDesign.com.

Chapter title illustrations by Richard Kendall, with the exception of the
illustration on page 67, which was done by Robert Butts.

Printed in USA

"Be reckless in the expression of the ideal, and it will never betray you. Treat it with kid gloves, and you are in the middle of a battle."

Seth, *Unknown Reality, Volume 2*

Contents

Preface

From 1972 through 1979 I had the privilege of attending classes taught by Jane Roberts, a world-renowned medium, writer, poet, and one of the most brilliant people I have ever had the good fortune of interacting with.

My experiences with Jane and Seth have not only had a profound effect on my personal life, but have greatly influenced my creative life as well. The writings in this book are evidence of that influence.

Rich Kendall
September 2019

REFLECTIONS

❖ ❖ ❖

Salem Possessed

In the late 1600s a very sad chapter in American history was written. In and around the town of Salem, Massachusetts, during the years of 1692 and 1693, a series of trials were held during which a number of local residents were accused of practicing witchcraft. These trials resulted in the execution of twenty people, fourteen of them being women. All but one were executed by hanging. Five others (including two infant children) died in prison.

These events have always held a certain fascination for me, and while I have had the desire to visit Salem at various times, I haven't done so as of yet. Recently however, I started thinking about those trials again when I came across a book called *Salem Possessed*.

What caught my attention about this book was the last name of the author, which was "Nissenbaum," which happens to be my birth name before I legally changed it to Kendall.

Although the book was well written, as I started reading about these trials and the events surrounding them, it was so disturbing to me that I put the book back on the shelf without finishing it. But I did follow up on one thing. The authors mentioned a play called *The Crucible,* which was a dramatization of the trials that took place in Salem during that two-year period. I had the impulse to find out more about this play and after a little research I found out that the play had been a huge success on Broadway in the 1950s and years later was turned into a movie that ended up winning an Academy Award for Best Screenplay. Now that my curiosity about the play was satisfied, I set aside my preoccupation with the Salem Witch Trials and moved on to other things.

But sometimes, when one tries to push something down and not deal with it, then like some jack-in-the-box it has a way of popping back up. What happened to me the other day while taking my morning walk is a perfect example of one of those times.

I like to take brisk walks at least once a day and I usually follow the same route, which at one point goes by a high school which is adjacent to a large parking lot. There's a fence around this parking lot and there's always lots of debris around this fence. This particular morning I saw a typewritten piece of paper sticking out from one of the spaces in the fence. For some reason I was curious as to what was written on this piece of paper and removed it from the fence, though inadvertently tore it while doing so. Although the paper now was torn and had dirt stains on it, I was able to tape it back together and read the contents.

The heading on the paper was "English 2 Honors, Period 3 A," and further down it said "Journals for Act 4," followed by some excerpts from a play, with the names of some of the characters. Although the name of the play was never mentioned, I read the excerpts, which spoke of these girls being accused of witchcraft.

I then went online and downloaded the text to *The Crucible* and sure enough, the names of the characters in *The Crucible* were the same as the names of the characters on the piece of paper I had just removed from the fence.

Now if one likes to think in terms of odds or statistics, I don't think one could calculate what the odds would be of finding a piece of paper wedged in an opening in a fence which contained excerpts from a play I had just been researching.

The events that occurred in Salem demonstrate what can happen when superstition and beliefs in evil are allowed to run rampant.

When we allow any group of people to be demonized without pushing back, we create conditions that become ripe for the most deplorable and inhumane actions to take place. Such actions are occurring today as immigrants and people who seem different than "us," have become the new demons. We may not build gallows and hang such folks, as was done in Salem, but the cages and prisons we put them in aren't much better.

Addendum

I finished this piece about Salem late in the afternoon, and decided I would take a break and watch a movie. I chose *Regarding Henry*, starring Harrison Ford and Annette Bening. I had seen this movie before but felt like watching it again.

Often, after watching a movie, I pick one of the actors from the film and go to *International Movie Database* (imdb.com) to see what other movies he or she may have appeared in, and to learn a little bit more about their personal lives.

So after watching *Regarding Henry* I went to imdb.com and plugged in the name of Rebecca Miller. She had a minor role in the movie, and I didn't have any particular conscious reason for choosing her; I was just going along with my impulses. As I began to read about her I came across the following:

"She met her future husband, Daniel Day-Lewis, at her father's house while the two men were preparing the film version of Miller's play, THE CRUCIBLE. The "Miller" they were referring to was Arthur Miller, and the fact that Rebecca Miller was his daughter was something I had no idea of when I picked her name to enter into the imdb.com database.

❖ ❖ ❖

World Views

There are certain subjects that appear throughout the Seth material, which like orchestral themes play over and over again. I'd like to briefly discuss a few of those themes. The first one concerns how we perceive mankind in general.

For the past two thousand years the human race has viewed itself as a tainted and flawed species. Symbolically, we have put a mark on our foreheads that states "Born In Sin, Unworthy Creatures, Approach With Caution." Such beliefs create a very poor backdrop from which to conduct our lives here on earth.

As long as we believe that greed, selfish desire, and violent impulses are intrinsic elements of human nature, we are like a runner who saddles himself with a hundred pound weight at the start of a race. And while I don't think our journey here on earth is like a race, our beliefs dictate how "heavy" a load we carry as we move through our lives.

The time has come for us to embrace a new vision as to what it means to be human. Let us cast out the old tales of treachery and betrayal, and pledge to ourselves to no longer be bound by what has gone before. Let us adopt a new vision that says our intrinsic nature is one of love, of good intent, and of caring for others. I don't think the struggle within the human race is one of good and evil, but is at its core a struggle with our beliefs about good and evil, a significant distinction.

The second topic I'd like to address is our beliefs about physical reality. The other night I was flipping through channels on TV and came across a movie about the life of Saint Ignatius of Loyola, who lived in Spain during the sixteenth century. In this one scene he was looking out the window and said the following: "How vile and base this world looks like compared to the sky."

Many of us still believe as Saint Ignatius did, that physical reality represents a lower form of existence, inferior to that which we think of as the realm of spirit. And while I hate to disagree with a saint, we are in the realm of spirit right now.

In an ESP Class dated May 15, 1973, Seth had this to say regarding physical reality:

Your godliness speaks through your creaturehood. It is not debased, and no entities took upon themselves the disreputable descent into matter!

Your souls are not slumming! You are not at the garbage heap of the universe.

In spirit's desire to experience a physical reality it transformed a portion of itself into rocks and rivers and mountains and clouds, and everything we see and touch upon this earth. We need to let go of old tales that physical reality came into being as a punishment for man's supposed sins. Physical reality came into being as a unique opportunity for consciousness to explore new dimensions of itself. So let's embrace that opportunity and leave behind any thoughts of the vile or inferior nature of physical existence.

Awesome Paint Job

One afternoon I was at a friend's house who was in the midst of some major spring-cleaning. Wanting to help out I offered to paint one of her closets. My offer was readily accepted, but it was also met with a number of questions as to how I was going to proceed. There was nothing wrong with any of the questions, but part of me interpreted them as an indication that she didn't trust me to do a good job. Seeing how I responded somewhat defensively to her queries, she switched gears and told me to paint the closet any way I saw fit.

As I was just about done, putting some final touches on the molding at the bottom of the closet, I heard my friend call out to me with a sense of urgency. I put down the paintbrush to see what was going on.

While I had been busy working with brush in hand, she had been busy going through a small mountain of stuff she had accumulated over the years, and was standing in the hallway with her arms cradled around a toy she had bought for one of her kids many years ago.

The toy was called Hot Wheels, consisting of a plastic racetrack and various self-propelled miniature cars, which would zoom around the track.

She then explained to me with great excitement that while she was moving the Hot Wheels toy to place it with the pile of stuff she was going to discard, she "accidentally" bumped into a box that was sitting in the hallway. When that happened, one of the levers attached to the toy became activated, resulting in the playback of a prerecorded message. And the prerecorded message was this:

"Dude, awesome paint job."

One by one we tested all the other levers attached to the toy. When activated, each one played back a different prerecorded message, but the lever she had "accidentally" set off, was the only one that contained a message with any kind of reference to painting or a paint job. We were astounded.

Now if one were to label this event simply as a coincidence, a random happening, then at the least one would have to admit that statistically speaking the probability of such a thing occurring would be astronomical. For one thing, the amount of stuff she had piled up was so huge that she was never going to get through it all in one day. Yet of all the items she went through that morning, something led her to pick up that Hot Wheels toy. Then, while transporting the toy from one room to the next, her body had to bump into a box in precisely the kind of way that would then activate the lever on the toy that would result in that particular prerecorded message being played back. I remember her mentioning afterward that she hadn't even recalled what those levers were for.

As for me, I could have chosen any number of tasks to help her with that morning; all of which would have had nothing to do with painting.

Later that night, while browsing the news, I came across the following headline from ABC News:

> An Indiana mother is hoping to preserve her son's memory by hiding his favorite toys, HOT WHEELS CARS, around the neighborhood for strangers to find.

So what are the odds: I write a story during the day revolving around a toy called HOT WHEELS, then later that night I come across a news headline concerning that same toy?

The official line of consciousness encourages us to view the universe and the events in our lives as the result of some random conglomeration of accidental atoms and molecules. But when coincidences like these occur, I think the inescapable conclusion one has to draw is that randomness is a myth.

In exploring coincidences, we provide ourselves with a glimpse into the inner workings of the psyche, where creativity at the highest levels takes place, as our inner selves in conjunction with others are busy fashioning and coordinating events that later appear in our lives as if by magic.

And while Rembrandt, Matisse, Cezanne, and all the old masters may have been exceptional artists, I'm pretty sure none of them were ever told "Dude, awesome paint job." But they probably didn't need outside affirmation in order to let their creative abilities flow freely, and neither should any of us.

A Simple Gesture

I received an email the other day from a friend of mine in Germany having to do with a funeral service she had recently attended. The service took place in Bavaria at a Protestant Church, and was conducted by a priestess; not a common occurrence in this predominantly Christian part of Germany.

Among those in attendance were some young men from Afghanistan. They were there to honor the woman for whom this service was being held, for she had been instrumental in helping them to start new lives when they first arrived in Germany from Afghanistan, which they had fled from to escape horrendous living conditions in their home country.

After the sermon, the priestess asked one of the Afghan boys, who I will call Arman, to say a few words. So Arman, a Muslim, went to the pulpit, read a few lines from the Bible, and then began to speak. I will now quote from my friend's email:

> Arman was a bit nervous and in the middle of his speech there was one moment when it seemed as if he was starting to cry. The priestess laid her hand on his back and gave him calm. This was a very special moment. I don't know if other people in this church had this feeling also. For me it was like a sign, we are all the same, Christians, Muslims, men and women. The Muslim boy and the female protestant priest in a catholic county.

The world is highly polarized today, with each faction trying to prove the rightness of their beliefs, and the wrongness of the other side's beliefs. This seemingly never-ending battle can only be resolved when we look beyond the differences that seem to separate us, and embrace the love that exists within all of us. That love was beautifully demonstrated when the Protestant priestess put her hand on the Muslim boy's back to comfort him.

In that simple gesture, in that "special moment" as my friend called it, all differences were transcended, all divisions disappeared, and only one language was being spoken: the language of love.

That language exists within all of us, and the more we can speak it in our daily lives, in our everyday actions, the more we can heal the divisions that exist within our world, and equally important, the divisions that exist within ourselves.

I am very grateful that my friend shared this story with me. A German woman sharing thoughts and ideas with a Jewish man about tolerance and the transcending of differences; how perfectly apropos!

Try Harder

I was going through some old notes I kept while attending Jane Roberts' classes and want to relate a brief exchange between myself and Seth that occurred during a class in January of 1973.

Every so often Jane would give us assignments where we would be asked to write down our beliefs about a specific subject, and the following week we would bring those papers to class where they were read out loud. This particular week I wrote a lengthy and very personal narrative having to do with the fears I felt during sexual activity, and my concerns that I wouldn't be able to sufficiently satisfy a woman in bed, and how hard I tried to do so.

After the paper was read, Seth looked at me, and in high humor loudly exclaimed: "TRY HARDER," bringing rounds of laughter from the other class members. Seth then continued speaking to me with a benevolent sarcasm: "Did it ever occur to you simply to let yourself go?"

He then spoke to the class in general:

> The tittering and the laughter is a good cover for the agony that he feels, and the agony sometimes that you all feel; and in the matter of your own beliefs about the nature of your spirit and the nature of your body and the relationship between what seems to be two entirely different things.

As I thought about that class, and the conflicts I felt as a young man, I began to think about young people today, many of whom no doubt are suffering in silence with their own brand of sexual conflicts, not knowing who to speak with, or where to go to try to resolve them.

While it's true that schools now have sex education classes where students learn about safe sex, and various diseases that can be contracted from sexual activity, we need a much more intimate discussion about sexuality. We need a dialogue that addresses our individual and societal beliefs about our bodies, our sexual desires, and sexual identities.

That discussion must begin with the premise that our bodies are good, as are our sexual desires (contrary to centuries of religious doctrine). That discussion must emphasize that our bodies are the physical expression of our souls, and as such, the body's desires are the soul's desires, and we cannot separate the two, nor should we seek to do so.

Below is an excerpt from the Appendix of Jane's novel, *The Education of Oversoul Seven*, which speaks beautifully about the relationship between the mind and the body:

> Honor your body, which is your representative in this universe. Its magnificence is no accident. It is the framework through which your works must come; through which the spirit and the spirit within the spirit speaks. The flesh and the spirit are two phases of your actuality in space and time. Who ignores one, falls apart in shambles. So it is written.
>
> The marriage of soul and flesh is an ancient contract, to be honored. Let no soul in flesh ignore its Earthly counterpart, or be unkind to its mate in time.
>
> The mind cannot dance above the flesh, or on the flesh. It cannot deny the flesh or it turns into a demon demanding domination. Then the voice of the flesh cries out with yearning through all of its parts; the ancient contract undone. And both soul and flesh go begging, each alone and without partner.
>
> Who feeds the body with love, neither starving it nor stuffing it, feeds the soul. Who denies the body denies the soul. Who betrays it betrays the soul.
>
> The body is the body of the soul, the corporal image of knowledge. As men and women are married to each other, so is each self wedded to its body. Those who do not love the body or trust it do not love or trust the soul. The multitudinous voices of the gods speak through the body parts. Even the golden molecules are not mute. Who muzzles the body or leashes it muzzles and leashes the soul. The private body is the dwelling place of the private guise of God. Do it honor. Let no man set himself up above the body, calling it soiled, for to him the splendor of the self is hidden. Let

no one drive the body like a horse in captivity, to be ridden, or he will be trampled.

The body is the soul in Earth-garments. It is the face of the soul turned toward the seasons, the image of the soul reflected in Earth waters. The body is the soul turned outward. Soul and body are merged in the land of the seasons. Such is the ancient contract by which the Earth was formed.

The knowledge of the soul is written in the body. Body and soul are the inner and outer of the self. The spirit from which the soul springs forms both—soul and body. In Earth time, the soul and body learn together. The genes are the alphabets by which the soul speaks the body—which is the soul's utterance in flesh. So let the soul freely speak itself in flesh.

The body is also eternal. The soul takes it out of space-time. The body is the soul's expression, and its expression is not finite. The spirit has many souls, and each has a body. The body is in and out of time, even as the soul is. Let the soul rush freely throughout the body, and breathe life into all of its parts. The first birth was a gift, freely given. Now you must acquiesce and give your blessing to the life within you. Trust the spontaneity and health of the body, which is the spontaneity and health of the soul. For each morning you spring anew, alive and fresh, out of chaos....

Making the Case for Joy

I happen to be a big fan of musical theatre, and although I was not alive in 1925, at that time there was a show on Broadway called *No, No, Nanette*. One of the songs from that show became very popular and was entitled *I Want To Be Happy*. The chorus to that song contained the following lyrics:

> I want to be happy
> But I won't be happy
> Till I make you happy, too.

Simple enough lyrics yet in their own way a perfect metaphor for a dilemma that we all grapple with. The dilemma I'm referring to centers around the question of how much joy do we believe we have a right to experience while others are still suffering. That question becomes even more relevant when the person that is suffering is someone close to us.

I remember speaking to a good friend of mine some years ago after he had told his wife that he wanted a divorce. They didn't have any children and his wife had built her whole world around their marriage. She even at one point told my friend that if he left her she would kill herself.

My friend, who was basically an upbeat kind of fellow, became enmeshed in a daily struggle. One part of him sought to express the natural exuberance and joy that normally characterized his personality, while another part of him sought to stifle it, believing he had no right to feel joy while his wife was feeling so miserable.

He would speak to me often about his situation and most of the time I just listened without telling him what to do one way or the other. One day during one of our conversations I told him very forcefully: **"Regardless of what your wife is feeling, YOU have a right to be happy."** I could tell by the look of surprise on his face that such a possibility had never even entered his mind.

Whatever the situation may be, all of us do the same thing in our own way; we make conscious decisions on a daily basis as to how much joy, or abundance, or success, (or love) we will allow ourselves to accept.

One other point I want to interject here is that none of this is meant to imply that we should turn our backs on those less fortunate than us, or not feel empathetic toward the plight of others. But there is a difference between feeling a natural empathy for the plight of others, and using that to deny or suppress our own joy.

Like most people, I've wrestled with this issue, and continue to do so, but one conclusion I've come to is this: regardless of what is happening around us, I don't believe there is ever a good reason to repress our joy. I realize this may seem a bit calloused at first glance, but viewing the issue from a larger framework I believe my statement makes sense.

Continuing with the theme of feeling responsible for the joy (or lack thereof) of others, there was another Broadway show called *Do Re Mi* that opened in 1960, which also contained a song that became very popular. The title of that song was *Make Someone Happy*. While I like that song, I must take umbrage at the song's basic premise, for *I don't believe we can ever MAKE another person happy*, and the very attempt to do so is doomed from the start.

Furthermore, when we take on the responsibility of trying to make another person happy, we are in effect telling them that they cannot find their own joy, and must instead rely upon us to provide that joy for them. Not a very empowering message.

When you allow someone to lean on you in that way, you take away from them the opportunity to find their own strength, and though finding one's own strength and solid footing can at times be a difficult journey, never finding it can end up being far more painful.

During the next week take some time to examine your lives with the following question in mind:

To what extent do you deprive yourself of feeling joy because you believe that somehow it is wrong to do so while others are suffering? The results of such an examination may surprise you. I know it did me, which is what prompted me to write this essay in the first place.

Your Own Power

As I was watching television the other day there was this news clip having to do with the pope, and as he walked by there were throngs of people who were almost in a frenzy as they tried to touch him, or touch some part of his clothing. It reminded me of a similar procession that took place when I was a young boy about nine or ten years old, and used to go to synagogue on Saturday mornings.

As part of the Saturday service, the Torah (which contains the sacred texts of Judaism) was carried up the aisle. As it passed, all the men who were seated would rise and jostle one another as they tried to touch it. To my young self this event seemed quite magical, but today as I think about these things, they represent something far different for me.

They symbolize how we often project our own power upon someone or something outside of ourselves, and then react in these extreme ways, not realizing it is actually our own denied power that we are reaching for. Once we make that connection we can then take that power back (not that it can ever really be lost).

The goal of anyone who sits in a position of authority or leadership, whether it be in the religious arena or any other, must be to lead people back to themselves, to put people back in touch with their own sense of power. The following Seth quote is from an ESP class dated July 12, 1975. This was the last class Jane was to hold in her apartment on West Water Street, before moving to her new home, Seth:

> I will be unneeded as all the ancient gods are unneeded, and gladly so, when you realize that the vitality and the reinforcement and the joy is your own, and rises from the fountain of your own being, and when you realize that you do not need me for protection, for there is nothing that you need to protect yourselves against.

One of the many things that made Jane and Seth such extraordinary teachers was that they were always trying to lead people back to their own sense of power. They had no need to magnify their own presence by minimizing someone else's.

As far as touching the pope's garments or the scrolls contained in the Torah, I think the following quote from Seth addresses this subject beautifully:

> You are gods couched in flesh experiencing crea-
> turehood, encountering experiences through flesh. And
> through accepting and knowing that you are flesh, you find
> the divinity that you think you have lost, because you look
> for that divinity in all the wrong places. It does not exist
> in places, in those terms. You look for it in exotic terms
> outside, somewhere else, whether it is in another city or
> in another country, or in another dimension of reality, still
> better. But it is within you now.

Interview With a Limiting Belief

RK: First, I'd like to thank you for joining us today. I know your privacy is very important to you.

LB: Yes. I've always felt that a low profile is the best way to go.

RK: Now why is that? Do you think being too visible will expose you to danger?

LB: Since I'm YOUR limiting belief, maybe YOU should answer that question.

RK: There's no need to get snippy about it.

LB: You're right. It's just that lately I've been feeling that you really don't want me around anymore.

RK: Well, I… If you really want to know the truth, I've been trying to break up with you for years, but haven't been able to find the courage until now.

LB: Are you saying you're breaking up with me? Right now? In front of everyone? What about all that we've been through together?

RK: Yes, we have been through a lot together, but that isn't a good enough reason to stay together.

LB: But where will I go? I've spent my entire life living inside of your psyche. It's the only home I've known.

RK: I know it's upsetting right now, but there are plenty of other psyches that would be willing to take you in. Just be open to that possibility and I'm sure you'll meet someone else.

LB: But NOT BEING OPEN defines who I am. I don't know if I can change after all these years.

RK: If I can change, you can change.

LB: I hope I didn't cause you too much trouble. I mean we did have some good times.

RK: I don't know how good they were, but they served a purpose.

LB: Just answer me this, I need to know: Have you met someone else? Please be honest. You owe me that.

RK: The truth is I have met someone else. She believes that being visible and out in the world is not only good for the mind and body but also is quite safe. Overall I enjoy my life much more than I did when you and I were together.

LB: I thought you liked being with me. After all, it was your choice whether to stay with me or not. It's not like I forced you to be with me.

RK: That's true. You never forced me to stay with you. I did so out of my own free will.

LB: (Starts to cry) But I gave you the best years of my life. If you weren't really happy why didn't you break up with me years ago?

RK: I've wondered that same thing myself. I think a big part of it was that I didn't believe I had the right to be happy. I also believed it was important to suffer, and that suffering was good for the soul. But when that belief started to change, I ended up breaking up with a number of other beliefs as well.

LB: You mean there have been others besides me?

RK: C'mon. You knew that. You just liked to make believe you were the only one. It made you feel more important. And you were important. Each of my beliefs is important. Look, we had a pretty good run and there's no reason we have to part in anger. We can still be friends.

LB: Does that mean I can visit at times?

RK: You can visit, but you can't stay over.

LB: Will you at least help me pack?

RK: I'll help, but with all the baggage you're carrying around we need to get started right away. Just yesterday I came across a whole bunch of subsidiary beliefs that had been sitting in the bottom of the closet that I had completely forgotten about.

LB: One last thing: You know I never intended to hurt you.

RK: I realize that, but you know what they say about the road to hell being paved with good intentions.

LB: Are you saying it's been hell living with me?

RK: Let's just focus on the business at hand. There will be plenty of time later on to speculate about all we've been through.

RK (Opens closet door and starts to sort through stuff and sees the following belief written on a piece of paper): "People will take advantage of you if you give them half a chance." Is this one yours or mine?

LB: I think it's mine.

RK: I can see this is going to be a long afternoon. Let's break for lunch. There's a small café up the street that makes these great burgers and also has the best fried chicken I've ever tasted.

LB: Don't you know that fried foods aren't good for you?

RK: You know what, maybe we should just continue packing and I'll grab lunch later.

LB: That's fine. Wow, look at this stack of old beliefs I just found hidden in the corner. Between the both of us we really did accumulate a lot.

RK: We sure did. We sure did.

The Woman From Big Flats, Revisited

About a year ago I received a complimentary comment from a woman named Anette in response to something I had posted on Facebook. This led to a friendship between Anette and myself, though it had to be conducted online since Anette lives in Germany.

In the course of my communications with Anette, I learned that Anette's family, and the family of Elsbeth (a friend of Anette's), had both lived in a small town in Germany called Schwaebisch Hall. The families became very close, as did Elsbeth and Anette. While there is nothing exceptional about that, what is exceptional is that I further learned that Elsbeth and her husband Heinz, who had moved to America in the 1950s, became good friends with Jane Roberts. Elsbeth met Jane in a rather serendipitous fashion as described in Chapter 11 of Jane's book, *The God of Jane*. In the book, Jane didn't mention Elsbeth by name, but referred to her as "The Woman From Big Flats."

Big Flats is a small town in Chemung County, New York, about ten miles from Elmira. And while Elsbeth and her husband Heinz were both avid Seth readers, they never witnessed nor asked to attend a Seth session. They were content to simply be friends with Jane and Rob, which I have a feeling Jane in particular greatly appreciated.

In August of 2017 I finally got to meet Anette when she and her sister Marlies traveled from Germany to the United States to visit with Elsbeth at her home in Big Flats, New York. It was also the first time I had the opportunity to meet Elsbeth. Due to Elsbeth's generous hospitality and the good conversations we all shared, I had a wonderful time. One of those conversations had to do with Kordula, Anette's older sister, and how she discovered the Seth material. Here are Kordula's own words, and with English not being her native language, there were a few words here and there I was tempted to change, but decided to leave it exactly as Kordula wrote it:

> In the 1970s, I found a flyer on the windshield of my car. On the flyer was a large advertisement made for Jane Roberts' book *Talks with Seth*. It interested me immediately, but in Germany the book could not be bought. It had to be ordered through a Swiss publisher. I put the flyer between

my cookbooks and forgot about it. If I could have bought it in a bookstore, I would have bought it immediately.

Approximately three months later, Elsbeth came to visit me and brought me exactly this book. At first I did not even know that it was the book from the flyer, but said to Elsbeth, somewhere I've encountered this before. She said I should read it absolutely, it was incredibly interesting. She ordered the book for me at a Swiss publishing house. A short time later, the flyer had fallen to my feet as I pulled out a cookbook, and I saw it was exactly this book which Elsbeth gave me as a gift.

As I read this account from Kordula, I thought about how sometimes a simple event (such as a flyer being left on someone's windshield) can later tie in to other events in ways that we cannot foresee at the time. And if somehow one were able to find the person who left that flyer on Kordula's windshield, no doubt the story would acquire more interesting connections.

At one point during my visit with Elsbeth I mentioned that I grew up in Queens, New York, a borough of New York City. Elsbeth then told me that when her cousins' family moved from Germany to The United States in the 1930s they also settled in Queens, in an area called Astoria. I found that bit of information quite intriguing considering the fact that when my grandparents came to the United States, also in the 1930s, they too settled in Astoria. I also happened to have spent the first two years of my life living in Astoria with my grandparents until my parents moved to a different part of Queens. I asked Elsbeth if she could try to find the address of where in Astoria her cousins had lived. After looking through some old letters, she found out they had lived on 45th Street near Astoria Boulevard, which ended up being only a couple of miles from my grandparents' house which was on 26th Street and 24th Avenue.

As Elsbeth continued to speak about her cousins she remembered that they had opened up a bakery close to their home, which subsequently became very popular. The thought then came to me that some of those freshly baked breads and muffins produced in that bakery had most likely made their way to my grandparents' table at some point, and probably more than once. The connections involving my family, Elsbeth, her cousins, Anette, and Jane Roberts, just seemed to keep growing.

One of those connections had to do with Maria Callas, the renowned opera singer. After watching some of her live performances on YouTube, I became curious to learn more about her life. Further research revealed that while her mother, Evangelia Demetriadou, was pregnant with Maria in 1923, the family decided to move from Athens, Greece to the United States. After doing so, one of the first apartments they rented after arriving in the states was (where else) but Astoria, Queens.

Another connection magically appeared when I was speaking with my friend Sheryl Mandel. I was telling her about all these synchronicities when she informed me that her father-in-law, who is an opera aficionado, had rented his Paris apartment many years ago to none other than... Maria Callas! And Sheryl's daughter for the past few years has been living in... Astoria, Queens.

My mind started reeling with all these connections as one just seemed to seamlessly lead into another. Seth once said that nothing exists in isolation and in light of all these connections that comment from Seth took on new significance.

Elsbeth's cousins standing in front of the bakery they owned in Astoria, Queens.

Another connection that sprang out of my visit with Elsbeth had to do with The Monastery of Mount Saviour, which describes itself as "A community of monks striving to live a simple, genuine and full monastic life according to the Scriptures and the Rule of St. Benedict."

The monastery was close to where Elsbeth lived and we decided to visit it one day and even attended a service. During our visit I was drawn to this beautiful life-size sculpture of the Virgin Mary and child Jesus. I then learned that this sculpture was created in France in the 16th century and then sent to the United States. The relevance here has to do with my reincarnational connections to 16th century France as detailed in my book, *The Road To Elmira.*

I began to feel as I have at other times, that all things are somehow related, alive in some kind of multidimensional webwork that we can only glimpse, but which makes itself known through connections and coincidences such as those I outlined above. I think the more we learn to pay attention to such connections and "coincidences," the more we begin to learn about the nature of reality and the mechanics behind the creation of events that are constantly being formed behind the scenes.

Reflecting upon my visit with Elsbeth, I think in its own way it was part of a larger event that began with Jane first meeting Elsbeth over thirty years ago. It leads me to believe that once a thread is established, it continues to weave its way through the fabric of time as new patterns emerge in a picture that is never-ending, always evolving, and constantly changing.

I want to thank Anette, Marlies, Kordula, and Elsbeth for choosing to be a part of this thread, and in the process, greatly enriching the tapestry of my life.

Danke schön to all.

Black & White

Throughout the Seth material, Seth has often spoken about beliefs, and how they play a critical part in the creation of our reality. With that in mind, it certainly makes sense to take some time to examine our beliefs, particularly in those areas where we are not satisfied with the realities we are creating.

When we begin such a review, we will inevitably find various beliefs that we may no longer subscribe to on an intellectual basis, and yet they continue to occupy space within our psyche. I want to discuss an example of one such belief I've been grappling with recently, but first some background information will be helpful.

When I was growing up I lived in an almost exclusively Jewish neighborhood. There were a few Christian families sprinkled in here and there, but not many. There were certainly no people of color living in our neighborhood.

Black people in particular were depicted in a very negative light. They were viewed as part of an inferior race; riddled with unsavory characteristics, prone to violence, and overall it was best to avoid "them."

I remember once when an African American family sought to rent an apartment close to where we lived. Our all-white middle-class Jewish neighborhood reacted to this possibility as if the devil himself, or at least a close relative, was planning to take up residence in our tightly-knit little enclave. Needless to say, these folks never moved in.

As I got older and had more experience in the world, I rejected these distorted beliefs, but as I stated at the beginning of this essay, while we may reject certain beliefs on an intellectual level, traces of them can still exist, often invisible to the conscious mind. The following event illustrates this point.

Not too long ago I had a job working at a local restaurant in the downtown area of New Haven. Like many downtown areas, there were always a number of folks hanging out on the street asking for money. As I left work one night I noticed this black man sitting on the steps of one the local businesses that had already been closed for the evening. He was smoking a cigarette and had his hoodie pulled partly down over his face. My first thought was, shit, this guy is probably going to hassle me for some money; a quarter, a dollar, or as the usual query goes, whatever spare change I might have.

As I walked by him he started to say something, but I decided to ignore him and keep walking. But suddenly, I realized he was calling my name. When I turned around, I saw it was Donald, one of my co-workers at the restaurant. He was taking a few moments to relax before going into the restaurant to catch up on some work that he hadn't finished. Now Donald was not only a great person to work with, but had many admirable qualities that were obvious to anyone who knew him.

This incident really struck me, for it showed me that to a greater extent than I had realized I still had prejudices regarding black people. While this event happened quite a few months ago, it was only recently I decided I wanted to focus on ridding myself of whatever vestiges remained of these lingering prejudices.

The day after making that decision I went to a local market to do some food shopping. Earlier that morning it had snowed, and as I was walking back home carrying two large shopping bags filled to the brim with groceries, I proceeded rather gingerly, so as not to slip on the ice that was beginning to form.

A car suddenly pulled up right next to me and stopped. As the car window rolled down, I figured the person inside probably needed some help in getting directions to wherever he or she might be heading. The driver was a young black girl, and she asked me if I was okay. I just sort of stared at her and she repeated that she was just checking to see if I needed any help since she saw me struggling with my groceries as I was walking down the street. I told her I was okay and thanked her for stopping and taking the time to ask.

A few days later I went downtown to do some shopping at a place called The Dollar Store. The Dollar Store is one of those places where you can buy certain things for far less money than if you bought the same items at a typical supermarket. Similar stores probably exist under different names all over the country.

After I paid for my purchases I started to leave, and this woman who had been on line behind me tapped me on the shoulder. She pointed to the floor. It seems some money had fallen out of my wallet when I was putting my change away. Now I don't think a lot of rich folks shop at The Dollar Store, so this woman could have easily chosen not to say anything, waited till I left the store, and then picked up the money. Instead, she chose to alert me as to what had happened. This woman (like the girl who stopped her car) also happened to be black.

The very next day I was going over to a friend's house and noticed this man shoveling snow in front of a small apartment building. He had his back to me and yet for some reason I had a strong impulse to say good morning to him. As I did so, he turned around and we both received a pleasant surprise. It was this fellow named Joe I used to work with at the restaurant who I liked very much. It really lifted my spirits to see Joe again. We chatted for a few minutes and I went on my way. Joe by the way (like the girl who stopped her car, and the woman behind me at The Dollar Store) is also African American.

It was as if in response to my intent, the universe helped orchestrate these interactions to assist me in changing the distorted beliefs that were still present in my psyche having to do with black people.

A few other points I'd like to make here. When you decide to look at your beliefs, don't be afraid of what you might find. It doesn't make you a "bad" person because you hold certain limiting beliefs. True spiritual growth requires honest self-introspection.

Addendum

I was finishing up this essay (doing some minor editing) when a friend invited me over to watch a movie she had rented called *Hidden Figures*. Based on fact, it tells the story of three brilliant African-American women at NASA, who were mathematicians and served as the brains behind the launch of astronaut John Glenn into orbit, the first American to circle the Earth.

As Seth has said numerous times, the universe is responsive to our intent. And while I can't prove the truth of that premise using any kind of mathematical formula, our personal experiences are the most important proof we will ever find.

Musings on Chapter 10

On February 5th, 1974, during ESP Class, Jane passed around a copy of her recently completed manuscript entitled *The Nature of Personal Reality*. She went around the room and asked each person who was attending class that night to read a few pages from each chapter. When the book was handed to me, the chapter that I was to read from was Chapter 10, which spoke of the potentially disastrous results that can occur to the psyche upon ingesting massive doses of LSD. Was it accidental that this was the chapter I was to read from? I think not.

In the sixties, along with my peers, I experimented with all kinds of drugs. But when I took a massive dose of LSD one day, I really ran into trouble. I had no context within which to frame the experiences I was having, and felt completely powerless in dealing with an onslaught of stimuli that overwhelmed my consciousness.

I felt my identity splinter into a thousand different pieces, and I couldn't get a solid grasp upon who "I" was anymore. It was as if "I" was a stranger to myself. The experience was so bad that I went on my own to a mental hospital in New York City and told them I needed to stay there because I could not function in the world anymore. They just snickered and politely asked me to leave.

My parents obviously knew something was up and sent me to a psychiatrist. I told him how there were all these parallel worlds and different versions of myself residing in all of them, and I didn't know who the "real" me was, and which world I belonged in. He told my parents I needed LOTS of help, but I refused to go back, and for some reason my parents didn't push me to do so.

But the mental agony I was going through continued. My consciousness was like a runaway train that I had no control of, constantly spinning off the tracks through what is often referred to as "flashbacks," and there were times I would sit on the bathroom floor with a small bottle of some poisonous stuff I found in the medicine cabinet and would pray for the courage to kill myself.

This was all pre-Seth. Years later, referring to what I had gone through, Seth told me the following:

> You made your consciousness into a monster that
> seemed to pursue you and so you wanted to escape it, but
> the innocence of consciousness eluded you and is only now
> returning.

The desire to "escape my consciousness" that Seth mentioned, led me to another drug, the effects of which were quite different than my LSD experience.

One day a friend of mine was over the house and had some heroin with him. That was one drug I hadn't tried yet but figured what the hell, I had little to lose at this point. I wanted to snort it but he said he wouldn't give it to me unless I used a needle and "shot it." I didn't feel comfortable with the idea of sticking a needle in my arm so he did it for me.

When that plunger was pushed down I entered a world that I never knew existed; a world where all the splintered selves and disjointed thoughts and unwelcome flashbacks just STOPPED. My consciousness swam in an ocean of tranquility that I never wanted to leave. Is it any wonder I became instantly hooked?

Even when I overdosed one day and my friends had to keep me up half the night by walking me around and slapping me in the face, the next morning I was back at getting high again.

The next logical question is what led me to quit. The answer may sound a bit Pollyanna, but I simply realized one day with unusual clarity that if I continued down the road I was on, there were only two possible outcomes: I would end up dead in my early twenties (as happened to friends of mine) or end up behind bars. It was at that time I decided to hitch cross-country (as I speak about in the chapter entitled "Go West Young Man" in my book *The Road to Elmira*).

By the time I started attending Seth classes I was no longer doing heroin, and through the classes was able to begin to get a handle on what I had experienced, and begin to put it in a framework that made some sense to me. Also, using Seth's ideas of changing the past, and the past still being alive, I have tried to reach "back," and assure that anguished self that things would turn out okay.

According to Seth, the past is not fixed in stone, but continues to live and evolve within its own time-space continuum. With that in mind, we can bring comfort and hope to earlier selves regarding a difficult time they may have gone through.

The more we can move out of a strictly linear view of reality, the more we can become aware of options that otherwise would never have risen to the forefront of our consciousness. And as we take action based upon that non-linear world view, then those actions will benefit our past selves, our future selves, and most importantly, our present self, from which all realities flow.

Roscoe Diner

As word of Jane Roberts' classes began to spread, more and more friends of ours wanted to join us. Unfortunately, at times the car was just too full to accommodate anyone else. This dilemma was often solved by Jeffrey (one of the regular class members from New York City) who would volunteer to ride in the trunk so as to make room for someone new.

One night as we were heading back to New York City after class, we stopped at a gas station next to the Roscoe Diner, a place that often served as a stopping point for us on the way up and back from Elmira.

This particular night, Jeffrey was happily ensconced in the trunk with the trunk door closed, as was his habit. It was probably around 3:00 a.m., and as the attendant inserted the nozzle and started to pump the gas, Jeffrey popped out of the trunk. To say the least, this was rather disconcerting to the attendant, who was visibly shaken. No one made any effort to explain the "Jeffrey popping out of the trunk phenomenon."

While I can't say for sure what images had crossed the attendant's mind while he had been waiting for the next car to pull in, some long-haired hippie popping out of the trunk of a car was probably not one of the images he entertained.

Perhaps the emergence of Jeffrey was like some kind of omen for the attendant, reminding him that no matter how trapped one might feel about their lives, there was always a way out. The attendant was about the same age as we were, quite skinny, with a very short haircut. My guess is that he probably grew up in Roscoe, maybe even close to the gas station where he was now working.

As he looked around at this motley crew with our shoulder length hair, I could see that he didn't feel very comfortable. We must have looked like some kind of alien species to him, and yet underneath the differences in outer appearances, I reminded myself that we all struggle with the same challenges.

Decisions he had to make as to what to do with his life were similar to decisions I had to make as to what to do with mine.

Insecurities that lived within him were the same insecurities that lived within me.

The desire to love and to be loved burned no less strongly in him than in me.

I think it would be safe to assume that he probably wanted to do more with his life than just pumping gas and cleaning windshields, as I also wanted to do more with my life than what my current circumstances reflected.

I wonder at times whatever happened to him. Did he get married? Did he have children, get divorced, open his own gas station? Maybe he became a famous author, and in one of his books he shared an anecdote about when he had a job as a young man pumping gas, some guy popped out of the trunk of a car in the middle of the night.

Decades later as I sat in the Roscoe Diner on my way to visit a friend in upstate New York, this fellow came to mind again. For all I knew, he could have been sitting at the table right across from me.

As we make our way through the world, each person we meet becomes a part of our journey as we become a part of theirs. And all encounters, whether they take place beside the Wailing Wall in Jerusalem, or at a gas station in Roscoe, New York, speak of the invisible bonds that we have yet to discover that unite all of us.

A Tuesday night in 1973, the Boys from New York at the Roscoe Diner (halfway to Elmira). L to R: Dan Stimmerman, Lawrence Davidson ("Lauren Delmarie"), Richard Wolinsky ("Will Petroski"), Richard Kendall, Robert Axelrod, Darlene Mayfield, Jerry Migdol ("Kurt Johns").

Taking the Plunge

From the time we are very young, we are taught that to solve a problem, our best bet is to rely upon the intellect. This reliance, or shall I say overreliance upon the intellect, adds stress to the overall psychic structure, often creating more problems that then have to be solved down the road.

Due to various limiting beliefs held by mass consciousness, we have conditioned ourselves to be suspicious of solutions that don't come from the use of the reasoning mind. As a result, we miss out on the help that is always available to us from other aspects of the self.

Recently, I had been dealing with an issue that while not of major proportions, nevertheless was proving to be a thorn in my side. As is my tendency, my first reaction was to use my intellect to examine the issue from every possible angle: upside-down, frontways, sideways, and every other angle which I could imagine. As the expression goes, I was getting nowhere fast.

So I suggested to myself that the answer would come to me in a different way. A few days later I had the following dream, but first a little background: I grew up in what are called garden apartments, which consisted of a series of two-stories of apartments all attached in a semi-circle. My family lived on the ground floor apartment and another family occupied the apartment above. In the back of the apartments was a large concrete-type field where my friends and I used to play stickball, touch football, and other games. This "field" could be seen from the back windows of my apartment, from which my mother would often call out to me, letting me know it was time to come in for dinner, or lunch, or whatever the case might be.

Now to the dream:

I was playing a game (on this concrete-type field I just described) and the object of the game was to carry a small round ball past the other team's players and place it upon a small ledge on the other side of the field (similar to Rugby). As I studied the defense, and the positions of the opposing players, I kept trying to find an opening to carry the ball past my opponents but couldn't break through. Each time I thought I had found an opening, the other team's players quickly shut it down. (There was also a small pool of water which one had to pass through to finally reach the other side.)

After many failed attempts, I paused in the dream, and thought to myself, "There is only one way to do this." And with that thought, I closed my eyes, held tightly to the ball, and dove into the small pool of water. Summoning all of my strength I started to swim, and within almost no time at all pulled myself up on the ledge and won the game. As I stood upon the ledge with the ball still in my hand, I looked up and noticed my mother and father watching from the back window of our apartment. They had big smiles on their faces, proud of what I had just accomplished.

As I thought about this dream, I realized that when I closed my eyes (in the dream), I was symbolically discarding the idea of using an intellectual approach to solve the problem I had been struggling with, and was relying instead upon what I'll call "blind" instinct, which far from being blind, led me to the exact path by which I was able to reach the other side and win the game.

A few days later, a solution to the problem that had been bugging me presented itself clearly to my conscious mind, and I knew that somehow it was connected with the dream I just related.

None of this by the way is meant to disparage the intellect. The intellect is a fine and necessary vehicle to be used in navigating through our daily lives, but sometimes you need to set the rational mind aside, close your eyes, and take the plunge, trusting that you will end up safe and where you want to be.

Seth spoke about the nature of the intellect many times, and in this class from 1979 Seth was pointing out to me some of the limiting ideas I had about people who I didn't consider "intellectual." Seth:

> Now, there are people who are quite involved with my ideas who do not know my name! There are people, believe it or not, on the face of the earth who are very content with their lot, and they do not know my name!
>
> They recognize the vitality of their own being, and they have ignored the belief systems of their times. They are ancient children. They may not read philosophy. They listen to the wind. They watch the behavior of the seasons, and they listen to their hearts.

They are the voices of nature and of the seasons, and they recognize their origin though they are not educated, in your terms. And their heart speaks information that their intellect cannot possibly interpret, and in your terms would they seem indeed ignorant. They speak words that would make no sense to you, Rich, for they would not be intellectual. They would babble nonsense that in intellectual terms would make no sense! They do not need intellectual concepts because they understand the nature of love and the nature of the soul.

Speak to them of Seth and the word is meaningless. They do not need me. They do not need my voice, because they heed the voices of the oak trees and of the birds, and of their own being, and let me tell you, in certain terms, I am a poor imitation of the voices of your own psyches to which you do not listen!

As we confront challenges that we face both individually and en masse, let's be open to solutions that the reasoning mind would say are irrational, impractical, and illogical.

What have we got to lose; hopefully— a large number of fallacies that are behind so many of the limiting realities we create and that fuel the fires of discontent.

The Universe in Part

In April of 1978, my friend Arthur and I decided on impulse to drive to Elmira, New York, to visit Jane and Rob. They were now living in what they called "The Hill House," on Pinnacle Road, which they purchased in 1975. We knew that Jane and Rob tended to be very protective of their privacy, but with Jane speaking recently about the importance of following one's impulses, we decided to take her words to heart.

When we knocked on Jane's door without any prior notice, she let us in without hesitation. We visited with Jane and Rob for about two hours.

During this visit, I was telling Jane how I hoped to be able to create my life so that each day was filled with peak experiences of consciousness, just like her life was. Without putting down my intent, Jane explained to me that her life was not an endless series of peak experiences, but was filled with the same emotional highs and lows that all of us experience.

I then went on to speak about how I wanted to feel part of a meaningful universe, and Seth unexpectedly came through. He looked at me and said the following:

> You are not so much part of a meaningful universe, as the universe in part. That is the next step for you to joyfully follow.

As I later reflected upon that statement, a number of thoughts came to mind. As "the universe in part," we would then be part of what God is, and as such, how could we have ever been separated from God, for how could we be separated from that which we are part of. And if we were never separated from God, then "returning to God" also wouldn't make any sense.

In effect, God would be each one of us; a compilation so to speak, of endless individualities all coming together to form a totality, and while that totality transcended each of its components, it could not exist without them. Other lines of thought began to spring up such as the following:

If we think of the cosmos as a multidimensional jigsaw puzzle, and each person as a piece of that puzzle, then each "piece," regardless of size or shape or color, would be essential to the construction of the overall picture. Each "piece" would be of equal value and importance, making comparisons between pieces in terms of superior or inferior meaningless. Additional reflections led to this:

As the universe in part, our continuing creation of our selves would be tantamount to the continuing creation of the universe. As our selves changed, then God would change also.

These distinctions, and the exploration of them, may seem to have little relevance to our daily lives, yet I think that the way in which we view the universe, our place within it, as well as our relationship with God, influences our everyday lives and behavior far more extensively than might appear at first glance.

There are other notes I wrote down after that visit that I'd also like to share. And while they are on the lighter side, rather than having them sit silently in a folder at the bottom of my closet (perhaps never to be discovered) I think it's better that they "come out of the closet." ☺

Addendum

My friend Arthur, who was with me at Jane and Rob's that day, owned a small vegetarian restaurant in Greenwich Village with his wife Ingrid. It was called "Arnold's Turtle." As a result, during our impromptu visit the conversation turned to food at one point.

Seth then spoke about Arthur's restaurant, saying that if he were to eat at a restaurant, it would be at Arthur's; but that he preferred his food more spicy. He said in particular he liked Arabian spices.

A few days later, a review of Arthur's restaurant appeared in a local paper. The review was overall quite positive, with only one negative comment, that being that the food "could use more spice."

Seth went on to say that some people are born into miserable living conditions because the food is good, and that the Indian cuisine, for example, was excellent. He said that while some of his lives were miserable, the food was good.

While I know I'll continue to reflect upon Seth's comment about being "the universe in part," his statement helped me to better appreciate the idea that the actions and thoughts of every one of us add to the overall picture of the universe. And though some events may contain a bit more "spice" than others, all are important, and all are worthy of distinction.

Shaking Things Up

The following event occurred in late January of 2018. I was sitting in front of my laptop computer eating an egg and cheese omelette. To the right of me sat a large glass of cranberry juice. Little did I know how my relatively placid morning was about to be turned upside down, literally and figuratively.

As I continued to eat my breakfast and watch the local news, I reached over to pick up the glass of cranberry juice sitting to the right of my computer, and inadvertently knocked over the glass. Like a miniature flash flood, the red liquid washed all over the keyboard, the trackpad, and started flowing toward the screen. I jumped up and grabbed some paper towels from the kitchen, and starting wiping away the mess as quickly as I could. I knew that liquid of any kind could do real damage to my computer.

After I wiped up the mess I started to type again, and as my keystrokes appeared on the screen as they normally do, I started to relax. That feeling however was short lived, as suddenly my computer screen went blank. I tried restarting my computer but there was no response. I then tried to shut it off manually, but that didn't work either. In short, NOTHING WORKED.

At this point, a mild panic began to set in. For one thing, I hadn't been as scrupulous as I should have been with backing up my data, and for another, if by chance my computer was ruined, I was not in a position to buy a new one.

To counteract these feelings of panic, I started to immediately give myself positive suggestions, telling myself that everything would work out, though the layer of fear beneath those suggestions remained strong.

Fortunately, there is an Apple Store in the downtown area of New Haven not far from where I live. At various times when I had a problem with my computer I would bring it to the Apple Store and they had always been able to fix it. So I tried to reassure myself, telling myself why should this time be any different.

When I got to the Apple Store, it was mobbed. It ended up it was "moving day" for Yale students, who were returning to school in droves. The customer service person told me I would have to wait at least three hours before being taken care of. I told her I would come back later, and stopped by a friend's house who lived in the downtown area. When I returned to the

Apple Store, the crowd had subsided, and it wasn't long before I was able to sit down with one of the technicians.

When he asked me what the problem was, I decided not to mention anything about the juice I had spilled, and just told him that I couldn't shut down or restart my computer. He did some diagnostics and then asked if I would mind if he brought the computer downstairs to examine it further. I readily assented, and as I sat there waiting for him to return, I felt like someone sitting in a doctor's office anxiously awaiting the results of some x-rays that had just been taken.

When the technician returned, he had his own version of x-rays in the form of a picture of the inside of the computer which clearly showed water having made its way to the inside of the computer. He showed me the picture and told me the water had done damage to the circuits. He then said they couldn't repair it in-house, and my only option was to send it out to an outside company affiliated with Apple.

Still trying to remain positive I asked him how much the repair would cost. His answer of $755.00 quickly obliterated whatever sense of optimism I had been desperately trying to hold on to. Relying on Social Security as my main source of income, I simply could not afford to set aside $755.00 from my monthly payments to cover the cost of the repair. The prospect of my not having a computer was quite upsetting, since I depended on it in so many ways.

Resigning myself to the reality of not having a computer for a while, I started thinking that I might as well just throw out my now water-damaged non-functional laptop. When I mentioned this to a friend, she suggested that I hold on to it. Knowing my propensity for throwing things out (I'm the opposite of a hoarder), she suggested that for now I store it at her place, which certainly seemed like a reasonable idea.

A few days later, I started to pack up the laptop to bring to her house, and as I was zipping my laptop case closed I had a strong and clear IMPUSLE to remove the laptop and vigorously shake it. This didn't seem to make any rational sense, but what did I have to lose.

So following my impulse I took the laptop out of the case, shook it vigorously for about five seconds, plugged it in, and hit the power button. To my great AMAZEMENT, the computer turned right on, the screen looked perfectly normal, and all my documents were intact, and I hadn't lost one byte of data.

I was perplexed (though quite relieved) by what had just happened, and sought to find a logical explanation behind this mini-miracle. Unable to find anything online to explain what had just happened, I called my sister-in-law who had been a programmer for IBM for many years, and she said she had never heard of such a thing.

This event brought up a number of things in my mind, the first one having to do with IMPULSES. We are often told that impulses should be ignored, cannot be trusted, and that following them can potentially be dangerous. Directly contrary to that mass belief, the Seth material viewed impulses in an entirely different light. Here are some comments from Seth regarding impulses from an ESP class in December of 1979:

> Now, when you trust your feelings and your impulses, when you learn to trust them, something very strange happens. They turn quite trustworthy.
>
> Your feelings and your impulses are your own private messengers from the inner self. Each impulse, to one extent or another, carries within it the initial power of the will to be that gave you birth. You have been taught not to trust your feelings and not to trust your impulses. So certainly in your experience it seems as if you cannot trust yourselves. But if I tell you, or if you are told to trust yourself, and at the same time you do not trust your own feelings or your own impulses, then where is a self in which you can put any trust?
>
> Your impulses and your feelings are innately now, your healthiest and your most spiritual touchstones in this reality. So touch them.

Had I not been exposed through the Seth material to this alternative way of viewing impulses, I highly doubt that the impulse to shake my laptop would have even crossed my mind.

The other point I want to mention has to do with the idea of authority figures, and by extension, the idea of "experts." The Apple Store technician

I went to certainly had a degree of knowledge about computers that was far greater than my own, and to call him an expert in the field of computer technology would not be a misnomer.

Yet here again I must credit the Seth material, for Seth had admonished us many times, that ABOVE ALL ELSE, we must trust the authority of our own psyche. Without that admonition, even if the impulse to shake my computer did enter my conscious awareness, most likely I never would have followed it, for why would I trust my own voice over that of an "expert."

The ideas in the Seth material have practical applications in our daily lives in all areas, but to be effective we must be willing to shake up the official versions of reality that we are presented with on a constant basis.

In the episode described above, the willingness to shake things up both literally, and figuratively, brought forth a wonderful result. So the next time you have a clear and strong impulse to do something (or to NOT DO something), trust it. You may be as amazed as I was at the results that follow.

Four Hundred Times

Sometimes I curse the fact that we cannot escape our beliefs, for according to Seth, our beliefs are the essential building blocks from which we create our reality. If only our positive beliefs were materialized, I wouldn't mind so much, but as Seth has stated, if only our positive beliefs were materialized we'd never learn the lessons we have set out to teach ourselves about how beliefs are the building blocks from which we construct our reality.

When I first read the book *The Nature of Personal Reality,* I decided to underline the word belief anytime it appeared in the book. I then counted how many times it was used and the number was over 400.

It wasn't that Seth didn't know how to express his thoughts without being redundant, but he purposefully used that word over and over again to try to get through to us the importance of beliefs, and the importance of becoming aware of the beliefs we held.

Despite all this, I do find myself resistant at times to working with my beliefs. Instead, I want to take that magic pill, that elusive elixir which will instantly transform my life and cure all my ills for all time. But fortunately, or unfortunately (depending on one's viewpoint) I don't think such a magic pill exists.

That doesn't mean there isn't magic in the world, but to whatever extent we experience that magic, we must realize it comes from within ourselves, and not from any outside source.

As far as being able to change one's beliefs, I have had my successes, but also continue to have my struggles. One thing I've learned is that I can do a million visualizations, about being rich for example, but if I don't truly believe I deserve wealth, or if I believe that wealth is a threat to my creative self, or spiritual self, then wealth will elude me as long as those beliefs remain.

Another thing I have learned is that in trying to change our beliefs we must be honest with ourselves as to what we truly believe. We may have certain beliefs that we don't approve of, or perhaps are embarrassed by, yet if we ignore such beliefs, we insure that they will continue to thrive.

So when working with your beliefs be grateful that the power to change your life is always within your own hands, and is not dependent on anyone

else, or any outside circumstances. That belief is the beginning of true freedom, and one worth repeating to ourselves, if not 400 times, then at least
until we really believe it.

Vereingung der Seth-Freunde

On October 31, 2008, I attended a four-day international Seth conference in Pforzheim, Germany. The conference was organized by Vereingung der Seth-Freunde (info @sethfreunde.org) and I was invited there as a guest speaker due to the fact that I had attended Jane Roberts' ESP classes during the 1970s. Having been to other Seth conferences, I knew I'd encounter a variety of viewpoints and interpretations in regards to the Seth material, as well as a number of different approaches to the exploration of consciousness in general. It can be quite challenging at times to listen to others present ideas that differ sharply from your own, and not have your buttons pushed. That is a challenge I continue to work on with varying degrees of success.

When I walked into the main conference room that first day I was greeted by a woman with the following comment, "Are you the one?" I was literally taken aback, and didn't know how to respond, nor was I quite sure exactly what I'd be responding to!

I then realized the questioner was referring to the fact that I was "the one" who had participated in Jane Roberts' classes and would be sharing some of those experiences during the course of the conference.

A few moments later, I found myself standing between two people who were discussing the notes that Robert F. Butts, Jane's husband, had inserted into many of the Seth books. One woman said that she found the notes totally useless and just skipped over them. The other woman stated that she loved reading those notes and thought they were an excellent addition to the material.

I then wandered over to some table where various translations of the Seth books were on display. I turned around and almost bumped into this elderly woman who was standing close behind me. Without introducing herself or engaging in any preliminary introduction of any kind, she promptly informed me that Seth was now channeling through someone in Düsseldorf. She went on to tell me that the resulting material was not as distorted as the material produced by Jane Roberts.

I politely told her that Seth had made a point at the beginning of the sessions that he would not speak through anyone else but Jane so as to keep the integrity of the material intact, and avoid the exact kind of situation this woman was now describing. In reaction to my comment she became quite indignant. She told me in no uncertain terms that she was seventy-six years old and knew what was real and what was not.

I was curious as to why the ability to see things clearly occurred at one's seventy-sixth birthday, as opposed to their seventy-fifth, or seventy-fourth for that matter, but kept such sarcasm to myself. As she continued to support her position with increasing vehemence, it became obvious that there was no point in discussing this further. I abruptly ended the conversation and exited as gracefully as possible.

At another point in the conference, someone stood up and proclaimed that Jane's health problems stemmed from the fact that Seth bombarded Jane with too much information, and that although Jane wanted to stop the sessions, Seth was insistent that they continue.

That statement, while untrue, was an extreme example of something I would be reminded of many times during the course of the weekend: Every person on this planet views reality in their own individual way, filters their experiences through the lens of their own beliefs, and then develops their own set of "facts" to bolster their world view.

As I was sitting on the plane going back to the states I started to think about that seventy-six year old lady who had looked me straight in the eye and told me that she knew that this other Seth in Dusseldorf was "the real thing." I wished I had responded differently to her assertions, less abruptly, while still feeling free to honestly express my opinion.

In hindsight I realized I had missed something very important in the exchange that took place between us. I was so caught up in defending my own picture of reality, that I missed seeing the reality of the person standing right in front of me—a person who at seventy-six years old still had the grit and perseverance to keep searching for answers. I missed seeing the courage of an individual who was still exploring the mysteries of life, unwilling to accept ready-made versions of reality handed down to us like some mass produced tube of toothpaste coming off an assembly line.

Whether Seth was actually speaking through someone in Dusseldorf or retired in Florida sipping Piña Coladas, I missed an opportunity to connect with a lady who probably could have shared some fascinating stories about her life; stories I now will never know.

Jane Roberts once said that if you begin to see people merely as beliefs, instead of as individuals who hold various beliefs, then you have really lost something valuable in your interactions with others. I had indeed lost something valuable, and while I had to travel a long way to recover it, the trip was well worth it!

Addendum

During my visit to Germany I stayed with Ritchie Dvorak and his wife Gudren in Nehren, a small community located within the district of Tubingen. Ritchie's wife worked in the downtown area of Tubingen, and dropped me off there one day so I could explore the city while she was at work. Toward the end of the day I discovered a little park just outside of the downtown area where I sat down on a bench to relax. A short distance from where I was sitting there was an outdoor fruit stand, and as the sun began to set and the evening sky grew dark, the lights above the fruit stand came on.

I then watched a steady stream of people riding their bicycles on their way home from work, many of whom stopped at the fruit stand to buy some groceries. There was also a small merry-go-round where children were laughing and playing. I suddenly fell into a light trance state as everything around me started to take on a magical kind of glow.

It's hard to find the words to adequately express what I was experiencing, but the sense of separation that one normally feels between one's self and the outside world began to disappear. I felt as if we all existed within a universal energy that surrounds us and flows through each of us, as well within all the objects around us. I also felt that the scene before me, while occurring in space and time, also existed in an eternal now, or as Seth has called it, "The Spacious Present."

Using art as an analogy, I think one of the common elements that exist in all of the great artistic masterpieces is the artist's ability to capture and freeze a moment in space and time, while simultaneously alluding to its eternal validity.

In that sense we are all great artists, creating timeless moments that are then framed in the context of space and time. But when we step out of that frame, even for a short while, we can get a glimpse into the true nature of reality, as I believe I did one October afternoon while sitting in that park in Tubingen.

Who Has the Answers Anyway?

In 1972, when I first started attending Jane Roberts' classes, I thought to myself, maybe, just maybe, perhaps in Seth I have finally found someone to answer all my questions, remove all my confusion, and tell me exactly what steps to take so as to create a happy and fulfilling life. And though I had not envisioned my mythical savior in quite the form that Seth took, the form didn't really matter.

With a body, without a body, tall, short, who cares. To be able to sit in front of someone who had answers that I didn't, who could see into my future and my past, this seemed like the opportunity of a lifetime. Wisdom incarnate, at least for a few hours, every Tuesday night. My thinking went that if I was patient, and asked my questions in just the right way, then maybe one of those nights Seth would take mercy on me, shine his magic light my way, and all my problems and hassles would disappear forever.

Now even if such a thing was possible, I soon learned that wasn't part of Seth's agenda. One of Seth's main tenets was that the answers we sought were within each of us, and Seth always encouraged us to listen to our own voice, and not to overly rely on him.

Listen to my voice with as much attention as I paid to Seth's? Who was he kidding? What was my voice compared to Seth's? The whole idea of an inner self sounded great in theory, but I wasn't sure where to find it, yet I did know where to find Seth: Tuesday evenings at 458 West Water Street, in Elmira, New York.

So I listened to Seth's words telling me week after week that the answers I sought were within myself, and yet somehow I just didn't believe it. So when I had questions, I kept looking to Seth, instead of looking for those answers within myself. The following examples from various ESP Classes are instructive regarding Seth's admonition to not overly rely upon him, and his often repeated statement that the answers we seek are within each of us.

July 18th, 1972: I relate an experience I had involving an awareness of thoughts that seemed apart from my usual consciousness.

Seth's response: "Your experience of last week was quite legitimate. It is up to you to interpret it."

November 7th, 1972: I ask Seth for advice as to what abilities I should be focusing on at this point in my life.

Seth's response: "Only that YOU examine your own beliefs about your abilities and that you do not cop out."

December 5th, 1972: I ask Seth if he has anything to say about a personality named Marguerite de Valois, whom I felt I had reincarnational connections with.

Seth's response: "Not now I do not. But I appreciate the reason for the question."

August 7th, 1973: I ask Seth about a dream a fellow class member (Sue Watkins) had having do with my song writing aspirations, and whether her dream was legitimate.

Seth's response: "I want YOU to comment on the legitimacy of that."

I felt stubborn that evening and later on asked Seth the following: "Would I be using my abilities any more if I created an image of Jane in the dream state, and then you came through in the dream and gave me the answer, as opposed to getting the answer from you right here and now?"

Seth's response: "Because if you are getting them in the dream, you will be using your own creativity, in your terms, better than when you look at this image now in your physical reality and get an answer from Seth that you should get for yourself."

In short, Seth was not going to let me use him as a crutch, for if he allowed that, I would never learn to trust my own inner voice.

In our society we are often taught that almost anyone or anything outside of ourselves is more reliable than we are. So we may run from psychic to psychic, or seek out the latest person claiming to be channeling some wise and exotic entity, but behind it all is the limiting belief that the solution to our problems cannot be found within ourselves. Here's Seth from an ESP Class on July 12, 1975:

> When you are afraid of your own authority, then you
> will accept almost anything rather than face the authority
> of your own psyche. A Mickey Mouse will do.

I don't believe that there is anything wrong with getting help from others, but when our first instinct is always to look to some authority outside of ourselves, then we are doing ourselves a great disservice.

One might ask at this point, in traveling to Elmira each week weren't you looking for guidance and answers from an authority outside of your-selves? And the answer to that question is yes. But the difference here is that Seth wouldn't allow us to set himself up as an authority figure, and over and over again directed us back to ourselves.

The Ultimate Dictator

There are various aspects related to the production of the Seth material that point to a remarkable intelligence that was at work behind the scenes.

For one thing, I believe Seth purposefully designed his material in such a way that new patterns of perception were automatically activated as the reader grappled to assimilate concepts that were quite radical, in comparison to how we have generally been taught to view reality.

I also believe that many of the words Seth chose to convey these new ideas carry "triggers," which lead the reader to stretch his or her imagination beyond the normal boundaries within which our consciousness usually operates.

Another factor indicative of the level of intelligence behind the material's production, was the fact that as the reader's comprehension expanded, so did the material. This characteristic prevents the material from becoming stale, and is why when we go back and reread a Seth book, it seems like (and literally is) a new book.

Another aspect regarding the material's production that is truly astounding, is the fact that Seth dictated a coherent body of work, consisting of thousands of pages of material, WITHOUT ONCE losing his focus or train of thought—despite days, and even weeks, passing between sessions.

Continuing along these lines, in the approximately one hundred ESP Classes I attended, I never saw Seth hesitate, stutter, or be at a loss as to how to answer a question a student may have asked. I also never saw Seth in a bad mood, or angry, or vindictive, or behave in a petty or capricious manner. I'm sure if Rob were here he would say the same thing regarding all the sessions he witnessed during the two decades that Jane spoke for Seth.

I think it is also worth noting that Seth's willingness to address the possibility of distortions in the material he was delivering was quite unique, and something that to my knowledge you won't find in other channeled material.

One last point I want to make. Because of the kind of people that Jane and Rob were, the material achieved a certain degree of excellence that would have been hard to duplicate had Seth spoken through someone else. And while Seth never said he couldn't speak through someone else, he stated very early on that he would only speak through Jane so as to preserve the authenticity of the material.

In my estimation, *The Seth Material* (including Jane and Rob's writings), is one of the most brilliant compilations of creative thought that have come down the pike in centuries. So it is only fitting that the circumstances and logistics attached to the production of that material, was, and is, in its own way, just as brilliant.

COUNTERPARTS,
PROBABLE SELVES,
REINCARNATIONAL
SELVES

❖ ❖ ❖

Mayan Memories

In 1995, I received a card and note from Angela Murphy, a fellow Seth reader who I hadn't heard from in a number of years. In the card she wrote a note regarding a possible life I may have lived as a Mayan woman. Here's a copy of the card and note she sent me:

Tue March 7 '95

Hi R.K.

I don't know why, but I saw this card and thought of you. Have you ever had any sensation of being out of the Mayan culture? I have.

About twenty years before Angela's note, Sue Watkins wrote the following to me:

> I was thinking about yellow jackets and why they are invading the house. Suddenly, I saw you as a woman in a field of some kind of knee-high crop, like corn, only the word was maize. It was high up in the mountains in the Incan empire of Peru, only you were of Mayan descent.
>
> The crops were planted in this amazing pattern of circles, a ritual crop pattern. You were dressed in layers of coarse but soft colored (tawny) cloth stuff. You were bent over doing some thing in this maize when you suddenly straightened up, hands on your face, screaming. A swarm or nest of hornets rose up from just behind you, and got all over you. I didn't see the end, but I know you didn't even have a chance to run. Some fun, eh keed?

Indian Dreams

One night during class, Jane Roberts looked at me and unrelated to anything that was happening in class at the moment, said, "Rich, you were an Indian." That's all she said, and then continued on with class. I didn't ask her anything more about her statement but have often felt strong connections with American Indians at various times in my life. Some years later, I had this very vivid dream:

In the dream I was an American Indian, sitting upon a horse, and looking out upon a large field. Then seemingly out of nowhere, another Indian came riding up swiftly behind me, and before I had a chance to react, he struck me squarely on the head with his tomahawk. I fell off my horse and my body started rolling on the ground though I was not in any pain.

In the next instant I found myself sitting up in the dream, and though my eyes were closed (in the dream) a picture began to form within my mind. The picture was of a beautiful blue nighttime sky, with the moon shining in the background. I then opened my eyes (in the dream) and when I did so I saw and felt a woman's arms and hands reaching across my body from behind. There was an incredible sense of healing energy that began to emanate from the softness and warmth of her hands, and strong feelings of peace began to fill my entire body. I instinctively knew I wasn't supposed to look behind me to see her image, and I didn't.

Still dreaming, I wondered in the dream if I was dead, and had the impulse to open my eyes (in this reality) but was a bit concerned that when I did I would find out that I really had died. I was also resistant to opening my eyes because I didn't want to lose the feelings of tranquility I was experiencing in the dream.

I then opened my eyes (in this reality) and the feelings of peace I had experienced in the dream carried over for a short time into this reality. Also, as I felt the folds of the blanket that lay by my side in the bed, they felt exactly like the woman's arms and hands in the dream. This sensation lasted only a few seconds after which I fully awoke, and the folds of the blanket once more became simply the folds of a blanket.

One last thing I remember is that someone was reciting a poem of some sort though I knew it was more than just a poem. The only two lines I can remember are these: "Private message. Private gratitude."

Knight at the Museum

Another evening, also unrelated to what was going on in class, Jane looked at me and stated, "Rich, you were a knight." That was it. No preface, no follow-up, just that standalone statement. And I didn't ask her anything further about it.

A few weeks later I purchased a new pair of shoes. The shape of the upper part of the shoe was very strange. Rather than being tapered in any kind of way to provide a snug fit for one's foot, it was shaped like a large oversized square. I didn't know why I had the impulse to buy such an odd looking pair of shoes, but despite their odd look I did so.

A short time later I went to the Museum of Natural History in New York City with a friend. While wandering around, we came upon a life-size replica of a knight sitting on a horse. The knight had only one shoe on, but the shoe was IDENTICAL to the shoes I had just bought. I was quite stunned, but reminded once again of how past, present, and future lives weave in and out of time, surprising us at times like some stranger that suddenly turns up at our door, and though we have never seen him before, has a familiarity we cannot deny.

A Gay Visitor

There are times when other aspects of ourselves, without warning, suddenly appear in this reality. Jane Roberts used to call these appearances "bleed-throughs." These bleed-throughs can show themselves in various ways, sometimes quite subtle. This particular night however, when I was in my late teens at a party at a friend's house in the Bronx, there was nothing subtle about the self whose presence I suddenly felt.

As part of a prank, I had dressed up as a woman to pull a ruse on an old friend, who would be arriving later in the evening. But as the drama

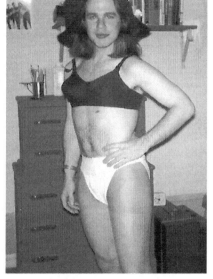

unfolded, the players became all too real. I felt the strong presence of a gay man within me, and began viewing the world as he did. I was experiencing the feelings of this probable self as if they were my own. At the same time I became acutely aware of the contrasts between us.

This other self had no need or inclination to hide his flamboyant nature. He felt totally free to spontaneously express himself without fearing that doing so might evoke ridicule or criticism from others.

My actions on the other hand were often strongly rooted within the confines of society's unwritten rules of acceptable behavior. It was as if year after year I had kept putting on more and more layers of unnecessary clothing until I was so weighed down by all this extraneous matter that spontaneous movement became almost impossible to achieve.

My good friend Emmy van Swaaij from the Netherlands has often experienced what she describes as "peeking along" with other aspects of herself. I like the phrase "peeking along," because even a glimpse into the ways in which other aspects of ourselves view reality can help us see the limitations in our own world view, and our own behavior.

And next time he visits, I'll put on a sparkly pink and white dress in honor of his visit, as we share the same stage for a short period of time. Perhaps we can even stand in front of the mirror and sing *I Feel Pretty* as was done by Maria in *West Side Story*. A multidimensional duet for the ages.

Rich Kendall and Lawrence Davidson

California Dreamin'

There is a version of myself that lives on the California coast.

I don't know how long he has lived there, but he likes to take walks at night as cool ocean breezes blow across his face and caress his skin.

He often eats out at local seafood restaurants and is particularly fond of Filet of Sole Almondine. He has a girlfriend but likes his independence. He's just not ready yet to make any long-term commitments. He doesn't know of my existence, and I think it's probably better that way.

Rich Kendall, Carlsbad ,California 1999

This other version of myself works in the movie industry as a film editor, having been introduced to his craft by his uncle, who was a well-respected film editor back in the days when footage was spliced together by hand, using tape or glue.

Unlike me, he does not tie his mind up in knots obsessing about the larger philosophical questions of life, but contentedly focuses on each day.

He sometimes feels depressed with no apparent reason, but that's my fault, for the intensity of my low periods can't help but bleed into his consciousness at times. But he doesn't stay depressed for long.

He's very liberal in his thinking; we have that in common. And while he doesn't stick his head in the sand, he doesn't rage against the injustices of the world as I do. He has a poster on his bedroom wall that says, "The World Is Too Big To Fight, So Make Peace Within Yourself."

He once almost caught a glimpse of me when I was vacationing in Carlsbad. He was having dinner with his girlfriend and glanced out the window just as I was walking by. The incident was quickly forgotten by him, though I have wondered at times what would have happened if I walked into the restaurant and introduced myself.

I like this version of myself. He is a kind and considerate person, and far more patient than I am. But I cannot become him any more than he can become me. Yet just knowing that he exists enriches my life in ways that are hard to explain.

I dream of him sometimes. The other night I dreamed that he finally decided to ask his girlfriend to marry him and she readily agreed. While I don't expect to be receiving a wedding invitation in the mail, I felt the dream was important.

Despite the miles that separate us, we share a certain kind of closeness that defies

Rich Kendall, Carlsbad, California 1999

space and time. It's possible we will meet one day, and if that happens there will be a flash of recognition, followed by his question as to whether we have met before. But unlike me, he will not play the scene over and over again in his mind, searching for the hidden meanings of our brief encounter. He will go back to enjoying his daily life; and I wouldn't have it any other way.

Counterpoint and Counterparts

I recently read a biography of Cole Porter, and felt a distinct connection with the well-known songwriter. The word "counterpart" came to mind.

One of the activities I engage in is writing songs. Though musically I am worlds away from the talents and abilities that Cole Porter displayed, I do wonder if at times I'm unconsciously drawing upon Cole Porter's "musical world view" so to speak, to help me in my own musical creative endeavors.

I am speaking here of something that goes beyond simply being inspired by the creative work of another. Jane Roberts' books relating to world views are pertinent here, and worth reviewing: *The World View of Paul Cezann, The World View of William James,* and *The World View of Rembrandt.*

As the book progressed there was much I disliked about Cole Porter, yet at the same time I began to feel a certain empathy toward him. He possessed a very strong sensitivity to the world around him, and to others, yet often sought to cover up such feelings through the use of an incisive and often satiric wit.

Mixed in with that sensitivity was a sentimentality that he didn't feel comfortable expressing directly to others, but found expression through his songs.

I can't say with certainty that Cole Porter was/is a counterpart of mine, but when we have a strong reaction to either an event or a particular person, I think there is value in exploring what is behind such charged responses. Our emotions are not arbitrary, but are meant to lead us to greater understanding when we allow them to do so.

Roads Not Taken

Roads not taken drift across the skies of my imagination. Most of them are too high up at this point in my life to ever make their way down to earth, but the following road is one a part of me wishes I had taken.

It's a road where a gypsy guitarist travels the globe with no strings attached, except those on his guitar.

Beholden to no one, he sleeps on borrowed time that never needs to be paid back.

The ghost of Django Rheinhardt moves through his fingers as Stephane Grappelli's violin solos play in the back of his mind.

He lives for his music which will never betray him; a faithful companion through all the ups and downs he may encounter.

His sounds form a perfect geometry where atoms and molecules magically come together to keep the earth spinning at just the right speed; and even when he hits the occasional wrong note and a star may blink on and off momentarily, there is always enough light for one to find their way in the darkness.

People often say they have no regrets, but as I gaze at this old guitar of mine that sits in the corner of my room I have regrets. Sometimes I can hear that guitar asking me why I cut short a journey filled with so much promise. I don't really have a good answer to that question, and don't know if at this point the answer really matters.

Roads not taken.

POSTCARDS FROM
JANE AND ROB

❖ ❖ ❖

The following postcards were sent to me by Jane and Rob. I donated the originals to Yale University where they are archived with the rest of The Jane Roberts Papers.

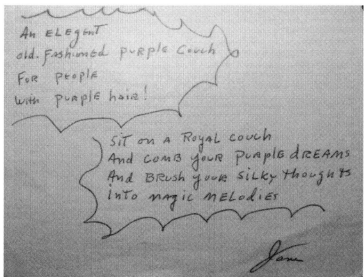

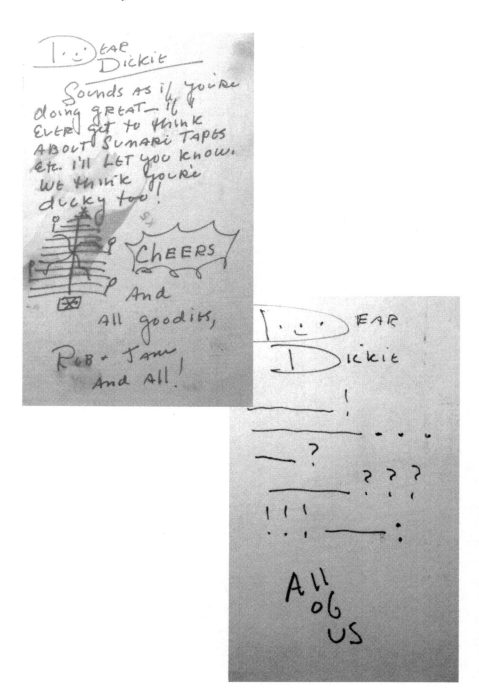

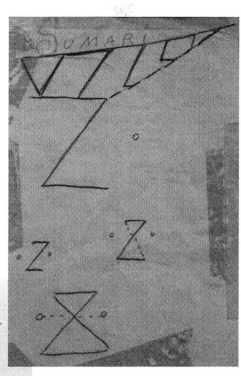

Dear Dickie —
WE REALLY
APPRECIATE YOUR
SENDING THE TAPE!
And tell SHERI
I FEEL SHE'S REALLY
doing WELL with
the CLASSES.
RICK, too!

AS EVER,

Jane

Dear
Dickie,

The Tree is the one
outside our front
window - sort of!
your card is my
FAVORITE of all the
ones we received
and we wish you
the BEST
Summer 1980!
    Love,
    Rob & Jane
        & Co.

MERRY
CHRISTMAS
Dickie

TO
ALL!
over

J.R.

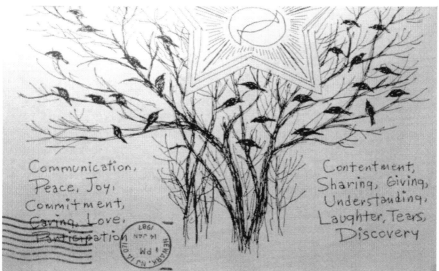

Dear
Uncle Dickie.

Your idea is
great - like most
of your ideas.
Its the Time -
(naughty word
I know)
But .. who knows?
    Happy Spring
    Jane for Rob

MAY 3/84

Dear Dickie:
    MANY LOVING THANKS FROM
JANE & ME FOR YOUR MOST ORIGINAL
SUMARI BIRTHDAY CARD! INCLUDING
THAT POEM. OUR BEST TO YOU &
    FAMILY - LOVE -
        Rob

YES, REALITY IS JUST A FIGMENT OF OUR IMAGINATION!

MISCELLANEOUS

❖ ❖ ❖

My First Class

As I walked up the flight of stairs that led to Jane Roberts' living room on January 4, 1972, I had little idea of what awaited me. Just a few months before, I had read Jane's book *The Seth Material,* where Jane described her experiences with Seth, an "energy essence personality," who spoke through her while she was in trance. I had never seen a medium before, didn't know if Jane would go into trance this particular night, and if she did, I wondered what my reaction might be.

As I reached the top of the stairs, Jane was standing just outside the door of the apartment where she held her ESP classes, as she called them. I recognized her from the photographs in *The Seth Material,* and as I approached her, Jane introduced herself and asked me my name. A simple enough question, yet from the brief exchange that occurred I should have known right then and there that I was in for an adventure (an adventure that continues to this day).

In response to Jane's question I told her my name was Richard. Certainly a truthful statement on my part, yet Jane responded by asking me if I was called anything else. Instinctively I said no, yet in truth, I was almost exclusively known by my nickname at that time, which was Dickie, and which I was trying to wean my friends from calling me. I was getting older and as an adult I just didn't feel comfortable with "Dickie" anymore. Jane accepted my denial that I was called anything else besides Richard and welcomed me to her class. She then walked across the hall to her other apartment.

Jane and her husband, Robert F. Butts, occupied two apartments on the second floor of this grand old Victorian house and I proceeded to enter the apartment where classes were held.

There were approximately fifteen people in class that evening, some seated on the couch, others seated on chairs, and a few sitting on the floor in front of this handsome wooden rocking chair, unoccupied for the moment. I parked myself in the back of the room near the large bay windows that looked out upon Water Street. I could hear the steady hum of traffic beneath me, and not far away I could see the bridge that crossed the Chemung River, whose banks were to overflow some seven months later as a result of Hurricane Agnes, creating one of the worst natural disasters in

Elmira's history. But tonight, as the river chugged peacefully along, I sat in anticipation, yet in anticipation of exactly what, I wasn't sure.

Jane entered the living room at about 7:00 p.m., sat down in the rocking chair, and began talking about some recent developments involving something called Sumari. Suddenly, without any warning, Jane took off her glasses, laid them on the nearby coffee table, and began speaking in a loud deep masculine voice. Her eyes seemed darker, and her entire demeanor dramatically changed. The facial structure, softer just a moment ago, seemed tighter, as if the muscles were more alert, more focused in some way. The most striking change was the expression within her eyes as she spoke. I had never thought about it much before, but realized at that moment that there is an intangible quality within the eyes of every person, which somehow stamps their identity as unique, and distinguishes them from all others.

For all intents and purposes, the personality sitting behind those eyes at that moment was not Jane. Seth then began to speak, easily and forcefully, talking about what he called the Sumari, and how they were gathering together from near and afar.

My two friends and I had just traveled five and one half hours from New York City to Elmira to attend Jane's class, so that certainly fit Seth's comment about traveling from afar. Yet I had no idea what

Jane Roberts in trance during class. To her right is Robert Axelrod; and behind her is Jeff Marcus.

Sumari was, though I was to going to find out a lot sooner than I would have thought. As easily as Jane had gone into trance and started speaking for Seth, she now started singing, powerful tones emanating from this petite woman which seemed to be bouncing off the walls, as she hit high notes and low notes with the versatility and true pitch of a trained opera singer.

When the song ended, Jane put her glasses back on, and various students shared their reactions to the Sumari singing that had just taken place.

When I was asked about my feelings concerning the singing I had just heard, I said that I felt I had been given a gift. Seth then came through saying that each time the Sumari sings or speaks we are indeed being given a gift, and that it was up to us to decipher that gift. I wasn't quite ready to decipher anything at this point, and was glad when Jane called a break. She got up from her rocker during break, and walked across the hall to her other apartment. It was understood that the fifteen minutes or so she spent during the class break in her apartment across the hall was her break as well; in other words, do not disturb was written in clear though invisible letters across the door of her other apartment during break time. How something could be written in clear but invisible letters I might have questioned a few minutes ago, but after experiencing Seth, and the Sumari, something being invisible and tangible at the same time seemed quite plausible.

During break, class members spoke in animated fashion about various topics that today one would place in the category of "new age." In 1972 that term didn't even exist, but that did not deter anyone from having experiences such as precognitive dreams, out-of-body experiences, past life memories, or many other experiences of consciousness that weren't part of our daily conversations. Jane reentered the room signaling break was over, though the room was still buzzing with lots of discussions, lots of laughter, and a feeling of camaraderie, though some of us had only met for the first time that evening, or had we?

Fred was a pleasant looking young man who seemed both friendly and intelligent as he participated in class that evening. So when one of the class members turned to me and asked why I was feeling all this anger toward Fred, I began to squirm in my seat. My immediate reaction was to deny feeling any anger toward this fellow I had never met, though in fact, each time he spoke during class I found my anger toward him rising. Then another member of class asked, "Why is Fred on trial?" and I had a feeling I was about to experience my own trial of sorts.

In the next moment Jane was back in trance, singing in that Sumari language, and motioned for Fred and me to stand up together in front of her. We acceded to her request and stood on either side of Jane as she continued to sing in those vibrant powerful tones.

Fred and I were facing each other as Jane continued to sing, and she then put Fred's and my hands together. As the singing continued I could feel the anger within me starting to fade, and I smiled at Fred. Yet secretly (I thought), I was still holding on to some of that anger. Jane, while still singing and still in trance, once again put her hands over Fred's and mine and shook them, and all the anger I had been feeling truly dissipated. Fred and I laughed as Jane ended the song.

Before we had time to barely blink, Seth came through, looked at me, and said, "Let that be a lesson to you." It was not said in a mean spirited way (no pun intended), and I knew the intent was simply to make a point, and I did not feel put down or demeaned in any way.

When Jane came out of trance, I learned that Jane, as well as a few of the other class members while listening to the Sumari song, had images of a trial, with me being the judge, and Fred being accused of some kind of adultery, or some similar kind of misbehavior. As the judge I cut him no slack for his misdeeds, and I later learned that the Sumari song was meant to evoke within us memories of these events. It was also determined that Pete, a friend of Fred's, and Jeffrey, a friend of mine, both who were in class that evening, had been witnesses at this trial. Bee, one of the local Elmirans who regularly attended class was supposed to have been the scribe at this trial.

I now felt able to admit that I had indeed been feeling anger toward Fred since class had began, but was defensive about it when called on it. Jane told me that it was no big deal, that we all get defensive at times.

Class ended at about 11:00 that evening, and as we began the long drive back to New York City we were filled with energy. It was our own energy, awakened from the events of a remarkable evening; a natural high if ever there was one. My friend Jeffrey started telling me how amazed he was when I was standing in front of Jane and singing along with the Sumari. Singing along with the Sumari? I honestly had no recollection of doing so, but at this point if Jeffrey told me that the couch levitated while the people were sitting on it I don't think I would have doubted it.

After a few hours on the road we finally started to feel tired. Few cars traveled along Route 17 at this time of night. The trucks however kept us company, as headlights played tag with each other, passing, falling behind, and then passing again. Our other road companions were the diners, rising up like some strange road creatures rearing their dimly lit heads. There was a lot to think about, and though no words were spoken, we knew our lives would never be the same.

Sumari at 2:00 a.m.

When I first started attending Jane Roberts' classes, my parents were not very happy about it. Having come from a traditional Jewish background, they simply had no reference for what I was becoming involved with. It also didn't help that I made no attempt to explain or share with them what this "Seth stuff" was all about.

One night while I was at my parents' apartment, I was sitting in the kitchen with a friend of mine and playing a tape recording I had made of Jane singing Sumari. It was about 2:00 a.m. and I didn't realize that the volume had been turned up far more than it should have been for that time of night. The recording woke up my father, and he stormed into the kitchen and let loose a rant about how I was becoming involved with all this crazy, dangerous stuff. I shut off the tape recorder and didn't say anything in response. I didn't feel there was anything I could say that would change his opinion of what I was involved with, or for that matter, his opinion of me. He then stormed back into the bedroom.

A few years later, my sister remarried and she and her husband moved down to Florida to start a new life. My parents shortly followed suit, even though they didn't have a job waiting for them in Florida, or even a place to live. They moved in with my sister and her new husband for about eight months, found work, moved into their own apartment, and never looked back. Following that impulse to go to Florida was one of the best decisions they had ever made, and they spent many happy years in the sunshine state.

As for me, I chose to stay in New York (well, actually, I wasn't invited to join them) but I wouldn't have gone in any event. Over the years, contact with my folks was sparse, but one day I received a note from my sister regarding my father. He had gone to a library book sale and on impulse bought a copy of *The Seth Material*. I never asked him what he thought about the book's contents, but the very fact that he went out and bought a copy of that book spoke volumes in and of itself.

What follows is an excerpt from the note I received from my sister those many years ago.

12/10/93

Dear Richard,

Happy Hanukkah and best wishes for a sparkling New Year.

Daddy went to the library book sale and bought a Seth book, which he is reading. Last night, he actually called to ask if I had a ouija board.

❖ ❖ ❖

The Morris Nissenbaum "Coincidence"

In 1987, my father (Morris Nissenbaum) had a coincidence that made quite an impression upon him. I asked him to write it up for inclusion in a magazine called *Coordinate Point,* that my friend Jan Sweeney was publishing at the time. Here is what he wrote:

> Dear Jan:
> As promised, the story of my dental problem:
> On Friday evening, August 1, as I was having dinner, a fixed bridge consisting of three teeth in the upper part of my mouth, directly in front, broke off leaving me with an unsightly gap when I spoke or smiled.
> Needless to say, I immediately got on the phone and called my dentist at his office but there was no answer, so I was forced to wait until Saturday morning when I tried him again, but still no answer. I spent the better part of Saturday morning calling him, trying to get his home number with no success and finally at about 1:00 p.m. I gave up and resigned myself to the fact that I would have to wait until Monday to contact him.
> Unfortunately, my wife and I had scheduled a flight to the Bahamas this Saturday afternoon, so with much reluctance and a resolve to keep my mouth closed for the weekend, we departed for Miami Airport. Once in the airport, we routinely went through the security check, my wife placing her bag on the track and picking it up on the other side of the scanner. As she did so, she noticed a folded brochure that said in bold print "FLY FREE." Curious, she picked it up and as we were strolling along to our gate, she opened it and inside was an application form in small print. Not having her glasses handy, she passed it over to me to read. I glanced at it and there was only one line that had been filled out.
> Where it said "name" on the top line was written Wm. Paul DeMirza, THE FULL NAME OF MY DENTIST,

whom I had been trying to contact all morning. I was stunned, and could not believe my eyes. We both dashed to the Delta gate thinking he might still be there, but the plane had just finished boarding.

When I saw my dentist the following week, and showed him the brochure, it was indeed his writing. He had taken a brochure, started to fill it out, changed his mind, and left it on the counter. He had traveled to Montreal that day to attend a dental conference and you can imagine he was as astounded as I was.

I still find it hard to believe that of the many thousands of people passing through Miami Airport that day, Dr. DeMirza left what seemed to be a message advising me that he was out of town.

Revenge of the Gumballs

I was walking around Greenwich Village one evening, killing some time before going to meet a friend, when I noticed this gumball machine on the sidewalk in front of a sweet shop. Gumballs are those large, round, colored pieces of gum that kids love to test their teeth on, often to a parent's dismay. But all it takes is a quarter and a turn of the handle, and like some small planet thrown out of its orbit, we watch with delight as the orb descends to earth, crashing against the metal lid at the bottom of the machine. For a moment we become the gumball's savior, as we lift back the lid and let the gumball fall safely into our hands. But a false Messiah we are indeed, for rather than becoming its savior, we promptly devour it as it collapses beneath the crushing force of our teeth.

Reduced to a mere shell of its former self, the gumball usually ends up sprawled on some sidewalk, left to suffer the ignominious fate of being stepped upon by endless anonymous feet, until some rainstorm washes it down a nearby sewer. Not a great ending for what might have been a promising future.

As I stood there staring at the machine, I decided what the hell, reached into my pocket, and pulled out a quarter. Just as I was about to insert the quarter into the slot I suddenly felt a clear impulse NOT to follow through with this. I remember thinking I could always use the quarter at the Laundromat, so why waste it on a gumball. I then thought how stupid that was, to worry about spending a quarter. So I put the money in the slot, turned the handle, and watched in triumph as the gumball made its way down the chute and shortly thereafter into my mouth.

Although the gumball was a lot harder than gumballs I had encountered in the past, as I heard it crack I felt a sense of pride that even though I was not so young anymore, my teeth were still strong enough to crush a gumball. There was just one minor detail to contend with: three of those teeth which were part of a bridge that had been affixed in my mouth were no longer in my mouth—but sitting within the wad of gum I now held in my hand.

Was this some form of poetic justice, the gumball's revenge for how shabbily its species has been treated over the years? Whatever it was, there wasn't much I could do about it at the moment. So I put the part of my mouth that was no longer in my mouth into my shirt pocket and continued on my journey to hook up with a friend.

One of the first questions that inevitably arises in any discussion about impulses is how do we differentiate between what I'll call "true impulses," which when followed will enrich our lives, and impulses that will bring unpleasant ramifications. I believe there is a part of us that always knows the difference. Whether we allow that knowledge to come to the surface, or listen to it when it does is another story.

I remember the quite conscious decision I made to ignore a clear impulse telling me NOT to put that quarter in the slot. In this case, the negative ramifications of my not listening to that impulse became readily apparent.

True impulses are direct communications from our inner self, private messengers carrying the results of probability computations that dwarf the capabilities of the most sophisticated computers. The mechanics of those inner computations need not concern the conscious mind, nor would it be able hold them. But the decision to heed these messages can save us all kinds of grief, not to mention exorbitant dental bills.

So what I learned that day can be condensed as follows:

Gumballs and impulses are not things to be trifled with, no matter how old you are… or how young you wish you were.

Head in the Clouds

I think clouds are a wonderful place to reside in. Clouds not only add to the natural beauty of our planet, and protect us from the sun's rays, but they also carry the rain that is necessary for the survival of all life.

Clouds trust their rightness in the universe, and know their worth. They know that just by being themselves they add value to all of creation. Clouds never entertain thoughts of self-disapproval, or take on feelings of guilt, so they don't have the need to punish themselves, or do penance, or punish others for that matter.

Clouds also don't compare themselves to other clouds. The Cumulus clouds don't think they are better than the Stratus clouds, and the Nimbostratus clouds never have an unkind word to say about the Altostratus.

Another admirable attribute of Clouds is that they never resort to violence, or start wars, and to my knowledge no cloud has ever lied, not even once, so what you see is what you get.

As I said, I like having my head in the clouds, and while my feet have no choice but to walk upon the ground, I've decided to keep my head in the clouds as much as possible.

And lastly, clouds are cool with people using whatever bathroom they want regardless of gender considerations. The only advice they'd give along those lines is don't hold it in. Ask any cloud and they will tell you that holding it in too long can lead to all sorts of problems. So when you gotta go, Go!

Sentimental Journey

There were flowers in the room, but they kept disappearing, and then appearing again, but no one minded.

Her smile once melted me, and I lay there in a shimmering pool of my own bliss, from which I actually had some difficulty emerging.

I once told her I didn't want to grow old without her, and she said I would do just fine. Her response made me angry because I wanted her to say the same; that she didn't want to grow old without me.

She once called me a thief—said that I had stolen her heart. But she forgave me. She always forgave me.

I remember telling her one day that I felt bad that I had gained so much weight, and knew that my youthful good looks had lost their edge. That night, she cooked me a pasta dinner with rich cream sauces, and for desert, made raspberry tarts sprinkled with bits of chocolate.

I was finishing a bowl of Cheerios and milk one September evening in 1999, when I felt the presence of another consciousness within my own. The words written above were silently spoken by that other consciousness, yet the emotions associated with those words resonated throughout my whole body as if they were mine. I was stunned by what had just occurred, and wasn't sure what to make of it.

For some reason I thought of Stan Ulkowski, who had passed away in March of that same year. Stan, with long-time companion Lynda Dahl, had started Seth Network International, a non-profit organization that published a magazine called *Reality Change*. Lynda and Stan had also sponsored numerous Seth conferences, and did a terrific job of leading people to explore Seth's ideas in new ways.

The same month that Stan had passed away, I started a new job for a company situated in Brooklyn, New York. Having worked as a paralegal for a Manhattan law firm for over fifteen years, beginning a new job represented a new beginning on many levels.

It was now November, and having been at my new job for almost a year, I was entitled to a week's vacation. This would be the first vacation I'd be taking by myself in many years, as a result of a long-term relationship recently ending. Not being sure where to go, I decided to be playful about it. So I went online, opened up a virtual map of the United States, and decided that whatever cities "called out to me," is where I would go.

I found myself drawn to a number of towns along the southern coast of California, and decided I would make Carlsbad, California my home base. I had never been to Carlsbad, or any of the cities south of Los Angeles, so I was looking forward to some new scenery and some new experiences.

About a week before I was scheduled to leave for vacation, I wrote a silly note to Lynda Dahl on the back of a postcard. It was one of many impulsive acts I had begun to follow as of late. In the note I told her how fondly I recalled that delicious seafood dinner we shared, and how spectacular the sunset had been as we sat by the pier. None of this had happened in official time, or in official terms, so I hesitated for a moment before sending the note, but then decided what the hell. I mailed the postcard and then completely forgot about it.

It was now the eve of my departure for Carlsbad and I was trying to do ten thousand things at once. The phone rang, and it was my former landlady, who had recently moved from Brooklyn to New Jersey. She was usually not one to stay on the phone very long, but this night she was very talkative. I didn't want to be rude, so I waited until the conversation reached a natural end, said goodbye, and then continued to get ready for my trip.

I made it as far as the next room before the phone rang again. It was a friend from California whom I hadn't heard from in quite a while. She had no idea of my upcoming trip, nor did I tell her about it. I wasn't really up for getting together with anyone, and just wanted to be free to follow my spontaneous leanings without having any kind of a schedule.

About thirty seconds after we hung up, my attempts to prepare for my upcoming trip was interrupted yet again, by another phone call. For a moment, I didn't recognize who the caller was. "Come on, you know who this is" was the response on the other end, and I realized it was Lynda Dahl.

I had forgotten all about that silly note I had mailed to her earlier in the week, and that's what she was calling about. She was curious if the note related to a dream I recently had, or if there was any particular story behind it. I told her it didn't have anything to do with a dream, and that I was just a silly guy who wrote silly notes.

We went on to talk about other things, and I mentioned that I'd be leaving tomorrow for vacation. She naturally asked where I was intending to go, and when I told her the towns I would be visiting, she paused. She then informed me that she and Stan had lived in that exact area of southern California for many years.

After we hung up, I continued to get ready for my trip, but couldn't help taking a few moments to think about the information that Lynda had just shared with me. I began to wonder: Whose memory did that seafood dinner and spectacular sunset really belong to?

As I sat at the airport the next morning, waiting to board my flight to San Diego, the song, "Sentimental Journey" kept running through my head. It was frustrating because I could only remember a few lines of the song.

The flight to San Diego was uneventful, and after deplaning and picking up my luggage, I asked someone who worked at the airport how I could get to Carlsbad. He told me there were shuttle vans right outside the terminal that left on a fairly regular basis. (Wanting this little adventure to be as non-structured as possible, I purposefully hadn't made any arrangements as to how I would get from the airport in San Diego to my hotel in Carlsbad.)

I didn't have to wait long till a van pulled up from a company called "Cloud Nine." This ended up being an apt description, for as I hopped into the van and it began to make its way up the coast, I unexpectedly started to experience intense feelings of ecstasy. The intensity of these emotions went far beyond the normal sense of relaxation or mellowness one might feel while being on vacation. These feelings accompanied me the entire way up the coast to Carlsbad.

As the van arrived at my hotel, I checked in, left unpacking for later, and took a long walk by the ocean. I made a brief stop at "Angel's Burgers," thoroughly enjoying my avocado burger, fries, and large root beer soda, and upon returning to my hotel room, promptly fell asleep.

I woke up the next morning a little before 5:00 AM without remembering even a snippet of a dream. After looking at a map of the surrounding area, I decided to visit the mission at San Juan Capistrano, which is known to be one of the oldest missions in the United States. The only other thing I knew about San Juan Capistrano, was that the word "Capistrano" appears in the title of a song which was popular in the 1940s: "When the Swallows Come Back to Capistrano."

I proceeded to take the local bus to the transit center in Oceanside, where I transferred to an Amtrak train, which let me off just a few blocks from the mission. As I entered the mission, a sense of serenity crept over me. And then, an odd feeling entered my consciousness—a sense of pride, followed by the thought, "I am glad the mission is still here."

The church bells from the mission began to ring and I actually shed a tear. It wasn't from sadness, but from a feeling of coming home, and part of me didn't want to leave. I wondered where these feelings were coming from.

I then went into the main chapel and found myself sitting alone in one of the pews. I heard chanting coming from one of the nearby rooms, and the sounds were so beautiful I felt myself being transported to a place of peace and calm. I then glanced up and saw a huge bas-relief, depicting Jesus hanging upon a cross. Large heavy nails were driven deep into his hands, and his blood, bright red and thick, was graphically portrayed as it flowed down his wrists. The sculpture jolted me out of my reverie. I then exited the chapel and spent some time walking among the gardens that surrounded the mission.

As I was leaving, I noticed a plaque on the outside wall that read "Vaya Con Dias—Go with God." Vaya Con Dias is one of the last lines spoken in the movie, *The Magnificent Seven*. I recalled that when I heard those words in the movie, they evoked a strong emotional reaction within me, as did my visit to the Mission in San Juan Capistrano.

The next morning I was back at the transit center in Oceanside, this time to buy tickets for San Clemente. When the bus dropped me off in San Clemente, I asked someone where the downtown area was. He told me to go to Del Mar and make a left. As I began to walk to Del Mar, the weather this particular day was without exaggeration, the most magnificent in memory that I had ever experienced. I felt connected to the weather in a way that I had never felt before. It was as if ever since my plane touched down in San Diego, I was experiencing reality in a different way, my emotional responses to ordinary stimuli being heightened in a way that is hard to describe.

I passed by a shop that had a big sign above it which read "Sentimental Journey," reminding me of the song that had kept running through my head while I was waiting to board the plane to San Diego. Those words seemed to be hinting at something that was happening during this trip that I couldn't as yet put my finger on.

When I reached the downtown area, I parked myself on a bench at the corner of Del Mar and South El Camino. Feeling like I was in a mild trance state, I took out a small notebook from my shirt pocket and wrote the following notes:

> I sit on a bench at the corner of Del Mar and South El Camino and mourn a relationship that never was and never will be.
>
> Images of former president Richard Nixon, who once owned a home in San Clemente, cross my mind.
>
> An elderly lady wearing what looks like a leopard skin hat slowly makes her way across the street.
>
> A man in a red convertible sports car drives by, bearing a striking resemblance to Stan Ulkowski, Lynda Dahl's former partner.

Suddenly, I knew my time in San Clemente was at an end. As I waited for the bus to take me back to Oceanside, I began to feel as if I was tiptoeing around the edges of someone else's life.

When I arrived back in Carlsbad, I had dinner at a local fish joint, went back to my hotel, and fell asleep watching old movies on cable TV.

The next day I decided to visit Dana Point, another of the towns that had caught my fancy while looking at that virtual map of the United States. The train or bus didn't go directly there, so I had to take the Amtrak to San Juan Capistrano, and from there catch a taxi. When I got off the train I noticed there was a bar across the street, and went inside to ask somebody if there was a taxi service nearby. The woman tending bar said there weren't any close by, but gave me the number for Yellow Cab of California.

I called Yellow Cab, and the dispatcher said there were no taxis available at the moment, but I should just wait there, and that he would call every cab company in the area to find a ride for me. I thought his determination to locate a cab for me was a bit odd, but decided to follow his suggestion and just wait. For some reason, a growing sense of unease was starting to gnaw at me, and after about twenty minutes, a taxi from his company arrived.

The driver was a young man with long hair that reminded me of my hippie days. I sensed there was something very kind about him. He asked me my name, and when I said Richard Kendall, he asked if that was the same name as the guy in the television series, *The Fugitive*. I said no, that was Richard Kimball, not Kendall. He then asked me in a joking manner if I was also a fugitive. I knew he was just kidding around and trying to make conversation, but the question was unsettling.

The taxi ride from the train station to the harbor at Dana Point was much shorter than I had expected; only about five miles. After dropping me off, the driver gave me a card with the cab company's number, and he wrote his name on the back, which was Herb. He said to make sure I asked for him when I was ready to leave. I told him I would.

Dana Point was quite picturesque, but as I walked around the harbor, the sense of anxiety I had started to feel after getting off the train at San Juan Capistrano started to intensify. Although I had only spent about twenty minutes there, I decided to call the cab company and have Herb pick me up. This would allow me enough time to make the 3:15 train back to Oceanside. The dispatcher asked if Herb knew where to meet me, and I said to have him pick me up right where he had dropped me off. He said Herb would be there in about fifteen minutes.

But after hanging up the phone, I couldn't remember where Herb had dropped me off. The harbor was fairly large, and I realized that if within the next fifteen minutes I couldn't get to the spot where Herb had dropped me off, we would probably miss each other. That would mean I would miss the 3:15 train. The next train back to Oceanside wasn't scheduled to depart until 8:15, which meant I'd be stuck at Dana Point for another five hours! In the frame of mind I was in, the thought of being stuck at Dana Point for another five hours just added to my angst.

All of a sudden, the feelings of unease that had been dogging me all afternoon suddenly erupted into a full-blown panic attack. I began to feel disoriented, and at one point I was flat out RUNNING THROUGH THE HARBOR, trying to get my bearings.

I told myself to try to relax, and started to recognize a few restaurants that seemed familiar. I then walked by a shop called Meara's Pearls, which

I remembered seeing on the way in. Using Meara's Pearls as a reference point, I continued walking to where I thought Herb might have originally dropped me off.

(I subsequently found out that Lynda Dahl and Stan Ulkowski had visited Dana Point many times, and LYNDA HAD BOUGHT JEWELRY FROM MEARA'S PEARLS numerous times.)

As I continued walking I suddenly saw Herb at the light right across the street. He saw me at the same time and started waving vigorously as if to reassure me everything was going to be okay. He pulled up and seemed genuinely concerned about me. He asked why I was going back so soon and I made up some bullshit story that he went along with so as not to embarrass me.

As we headed back to the train station, I kept jabbering about all kinds of inane things, and then, uncharacteristically, I started telling Herb about the Seth material. I rarely start telling people about Seth out of the blue, but Herb was really impressed by the fact that the material was being housed at Yale University. He said that fact alone gave it an aura of credibility.

We reached the San Juan Capistrano train station in plenty of time for me to catch the 3:15 train. The fare was a little over nine dollars and I gave him a twenty and told him to keep the change. He thanked me and again asked for my name, which I gave to him. I then asked him for his last name and it was something like Bocker. As I said goodbye, a strange sense of nostalgia came over me, and I felt a bit sad at the thought of never seeing Herb again. And that was my day at Dana Point.

As my Carlsbad vacation was drawing to a close, I thought about my experiences over the past week, and believe that Stan had borrowed a corner of my consciousness to revisit some places which held significant emotional relevance for him during the time he and Lynda had lived together in southern California. His own kind of "Sentimental Journey," using me as a conduit, which on some level I would have consented to.

While finishing my bowl of Cheerios and milk that September evening in 1999, I believe Stan and I for a few moments danced a dance of consciousness, which then continued during my Carlsbad vacation. It was a small dance; perhaps a minuet, and I was happy to let him lead. And while I may not remember all of the words to the song, the melody lingers.

Prove It

The world we live in is often obsessed with the need to prove, or disprove, various suppositions. Science in particular is governed by this approach, yet even in the scientific field there are exceptions to the mandate of prove or disprove.

For example, in the field of mathematics, Kurt Gödel, a renowned mathematician and logician, presented to the world a theorem bearing his name, known as "Gödel's Undecidability Theorem" or "Incompleteness Theorem." This theorem stated that within a formal system one will find questions that are neither provable nor disprovable on the basis of the axioms of that system.

One of the main tenets of the Seth material—YOU CREATE YOUR OWN REALITY—would fall within the parameters of Gödel's theory, being neither provable nor disprovable. That being the case, one has a choice as to how to respond to such a statement.

Some folks choose to believe that all events are preordained by God. Others believe that our lives consist entirely of random occurrences, the luck of the draw. Synchronicities are seen as basically meaningless, with outer circumstances and events baring no relation in any way to the inner contents of the psyche.

And then there are those (certainly in the minority) who do believe that we are responsible for all events we encounter in our lives.

As for me, at this time, I cannot unequivocally state whether the dictum that we create our own reality is true or false. But what I can do, and will continue to do, is accept it as a working hypothesis within which to explore the events of my life as part of my quest toward greater understanding regarding the nature of reality. And to share the results of that quest as best I can.

The Status Quo

A society's institutions often seek to define reality for us, creating a series of status quos which we are then expected to adhere to. Perhaps there is a fear that if everyone started defining reality for themselves, society would fall apart and crumble into a thousand different pieces.

The idea that a society remains viable only to the extent that there is unanimity of perception and opinion is a fallacy I do not subscribe to. I believe that when a society seeks to enforce standardized versions of reality upon its members, then such a society cannot evolve and grow.

Some questioning of current norms is usually permitted, but only as long as the questioning comes in limited doses and is not too radical. But when groups of people start questioning some of the very foundations upon which a society has been built, the backlash from others, be they friends, or family, or neighbors, or the government itself can be quite extreme. I understand that people often feel threatened by change, but for society to flourish, we must be willing to discard those status quos that no longer work, and not give in to the pressures to maintain systems that are not producing the results that we desire.

The Borg

There was an episode of Star Trek having to do with "The Borg," where individual free will was subsumed under a one-identity system. The crew fought like hell to avoid such an outcome, and I would have done the same.

Yet there are philosophies whose major goal speaks to the merging of one's individuality into a oneness that encompasses all. For my own tastes, I'm not attracted to the idea of dissolving my individuality into some amorphous vat of undifferentiated glop. Why would one want to dwell in a reality where one couldn't tell the difference between their aunt Alice and uncle Fred. Now I don't have an aunt Alice or an uncle Fred, but if individuality is to disappear, that wouldn't really matter then, would it?

Nature presents us with uniqueness everywhere we turn. I'm thankful for that uniqueness, and for possessing an ego that can look out upon the world with its own distinct vision.

I don't believe individuality is an illusion. The illusion in my opinion is the idea that we must rid ourselves of our ego, discard our individuality, and return to God. For one thing, while God may like us to visit every now and then, I don't think he's looking for us to move back home.

And though he may have agonized a bit when he initially set us free, or more accurately when we chose to venture out on our own, his essence is inextricably woven into the fabric of every creature, so we were never really separated from God to begin with.

Be proud of your individuality, bask in your own unique characteristics. They are yours for a reason, and I wouldn't be so anxious to give them away, regardless of what alleged bliss awaits us after disavowing this essential part of our being.

During a class in 1974 Seth made the following comment to a fellow who was there as a guest for the evening:

> Do not put your ideas of God, even though those ideas may now be fashionable, or liberal, in a package that is made half of Oriental philosophy and half of old Christian concepts that all result in the idea that you must lose your individuality in a Nirvana of spirit. For you

find All That Is through the understanding, the joy, the compassion and the experience of your own individuality.

So when the Borg approach, in whatever form, be it through a philosophy that seeks to annihilate individuality, or the pressure that society brings for people to conform and look and act and think the same, then like the Star Trek crew, don't give in.

Be thankful for the diversity that exists, and treasure your individuality. As Seth once said, God must love individuals since he made so many of them!

Script-ures

I was doing some research the other day having to do with the Old Testament, and started thinking about how the stories we read in the Bible are similar to movie scripts.

Sharing common elements such as colorful characters, dramatic twists and turns, points of tension and resolution, the writers of the Old and New Testament could probably have earned a pretty good living as screenwriters if they were alive today.

For a few moments, let's think of the Bible as a movie. We should probably give it a title; so let's call it "The Script-ures." We then need a compelling press release to get the word out. How about the following:

"Don't risk losing your soul, make sure you see 'The Script-ures,' a Catholic Church Production, opening soon in theatres of the mind across the globe."

While marketing and promotion are extremely important, the making of a movie requires the talents of many people, both behind, and in front of the camera. Of all those people, few would argue that the choice of Director is paramount.

Now if I were chosen to be Director of "The Script-ures," I'd change a number of the storylines. The first storyline I'd discard is the assumption that Christ was born to atone for the sins of humanity. Telling my audience that all of them are sinners just doesn't seem like a good way to start a narrative. Another storyline that would have to go is the concept that our time on earth is meant to be a somber affair, with the soul being tested through various trials and tribulations. While locusts and the Black Plague would be keeping with Hollywood's propensities toward special effects, the inclusion of such scenes might risk turning this epic tale into just another Grade B horror movie.

Next, I'd definitely have to bring in another writer to do a total rewrite of the Christ character. As portrayed in the original script, he's someone who needs people to praise him on a daily basis; needs constant reaffirmation that he is loved and honored; and needs others to pledge their sole allegiance to him. The problem here is that the qualities described above conjure up images of one of our current leaders; and it is essential that the protagonist in any kind of a drama be seen as an original, or the audience will quickly lose interest.

So let's find a new screenwriter to write a new script: or better yet, let each of us write our own new script. An original production for the next millennium; populated with characters that speak of joy, not suffering; of innocence, not guilt; and who base their actions upon the premise that our time here on earth presents us with unique opportunities for value fulfill-ment that would otherwise not be possible.

This new narrative, projected on the screens of mass consciousness, will bring returns that no amount of box office receipts can match. And when the Academy Award is handed out for Best Original Screenplay, we can all stand up and thank ourselves for having the courage to write a new chapter in the history of mankind.

Wealth Dream

The creative brilliance of the psyche shines most brightly in the dreams that are created each night, which always in one way or another reflect the beliefs we hold. I had been working on my beliefs about money and wealth, and had the following dream:

There was a large pole, like a telephone pole, on top of which was a wire-like nest with a black covering over it. There was a wire attached from the top of the pole stretching out in a diagonal direction upward toward the sky. All of a sudden, this "wire nest" began to move across the diagonal wire very swiftly, and I realized when it reached the apex of the wire, I would become very rich and would receive four black pearls, which would be very valuable, as well as some other things.

All of a sudden, however, I realized this wire nest had strings attached to my heart, so that at the exact moment the "nest" reached the top and I became rich, my heart would be ripped out.

I was frantically trying to separate these strings and broke a few but couldn't stop what was happening as the nest hit the top. To my great relief my heart wasn't ripped out and I was going to get the pearls, but had the thought that I would have to retrieve them from my shit. I then had this white taffy-type material I had to pull out of my mouth, which also was somehow connected to this wealth. The symbolism I think is rather obvious and in dramatic fashion showed me one of the limiting beliefs I held about money and wealth.

Let There be Light

In the beginning, God created the heaven and the earth.

And the earth was without form, and void; and darkness was upon the face of the deep. And the Spirit of God moved upon the face of the waters.

And God said, Let there be light: and there was light.

And God saw the light, that it was good....

And God saw every thing that he had made, and, behold, it was very good....

Well it's too bad God didn't stick with the program. In later writings in the Bible we find God looking down upon his own handiwork, having second thoughts about what he had created. (Those second thoughts will get you every time.)

Was the creation of physical form a mistake, some momentary lapse in God's thinking? Perhaps he was distracted while speaking with one of his angels, and as he momentarily lost focus he created the oceans, and rivers, and mountains, and all the creatures of the earth, only to say later, "Whoops, my bad." I think not.

If spirit wanted to remain hidden without physical form, it would have done so. Rather than denouncing physical reality as an inferior construct, we should celebrate it, and be thankful for the opportunity to explore this unique reality. Here's what Seth had to say about our foray into physical reality:

> Your spirit joined itself with flesh, and in flesh, to experience a world of incredible richness, to help create a dimension of reality of colors and form. Your spirit was born in flesh to enrich a marvelous area of sense awareness, to feel energy made into corporeal form. You are here to use, enjoy, and express yourself through the body. You are here to aid in the great expansion of consciousness.
>
> You are not here to cry about the miseries of the human condition, but to change them when you find them not

to your liking through the joy, strength and vitality that is within you; to create the spirit as faithfully and beautifully as you can in flesh.

The Nature of Personal Reality, Chap. 2, Session 615

Free as a Bird

The other morning while I was looking out the window I noticed a Blue Jay sitting in front of my garage and not moving. I went out and started to walk toward it, and when I began to get too close, the Blue Jay hopped a short distance away, yet made no attempt at flight. I wondered if the bird was injured. As I started to walk toward it again, the bird flew into a nearby tree. I thought its behavior was a bit odd, but was happy to see the Blue Jay was alright.

About ten minutes later I happened to look out the window again and saw the Blue Jay once more sitting near the garage. I went out and the same routine was repeated. When I got too close, the Blue Jay flew away. I figured that was the end of the story. But as I glanced out my window about fifteen minutes later, once again there sat the Blue Jay. But this time, rather than sitting in front of the garage, it was sitting in a patch of grass just outside my door. It sat motionless with its wings outstretched. I then knew that the bird was preparing to die.

I wondered what thoughts or images might have been present in the Blue Jay's mind. Was it reliving some of its great exuberant flights through the trees, when its loud squawking announced to the world the reality and rightness of its being? Or maybe it was remembering the delight of devouring some particularly juicy worm it had caught one autumn morning. And then again, perhaps it was simply focused in the moment, looking out at the trees and the sky as it had done a thousand times before, despite the knowledge of its impending death.

I don't know what the Blue Jay was thinking, but there was something majestic about the way it sat there with its wings spread out, acquiescing to the inevitable with grace and dignity. I went back into the house and about five minutes later when I looked out the window I saw the bird lying on its side. It obviously had passed over.

I thought about how this amazing creature, this unique materialization of consciousness had lived its life. During its lifetime it trusted its instincts without question. The Blue Jay never worried it might be headed in the wrong direction, or making a mistake. It just flew.

Holding the Blue Jay gently in my hands I walked toward the back of the house and placed it in the middle of some tall grass. I thought the spot

I chose would be a perfect place for it to REST IN PEACE. Yet as soon as that cliché crossed my mind I realized it didn't fit. Resting in peace was not what characterized the life of that Blue Jay, nor would it characterize its life after its death.

I thanked the Blue Jay for sharing its last moments on earth with me, and as I wondered what new skies it was already soaring through, another cliché came to mind which fit a lot better: FREE AS A BIRD.

Memories of Jane Roberts

A presentation I gave during a Seth Conference held in Seaside, Oregon, 1996

I want to tell you about a woman I knew who grew up on welfare, was kicked out of college, went cross-country on a motorcycle, married and divorced three years later, smoked, drank wine and beer, and at times swore like a sailor. Her name was Jane Roberts. Shortly before Jane died, she told Rob, "DON'T LET THEM MAKE A GOD OUT OF ME." So I hope that by providing some details of Jane's personal life, both before and after Seth emerged, you will be able to see her more clearly as the very human being she was.

Jane was born in 1929 and grew up in Saratoga Springs, NY. Her parents divorced when she was three years old, and Jane lived with her mother, who was an invalid. Those early years had their share of difficulties.

> "I once tried to poison the welfare lady," Jane recalls. "I took Brillo and Comet and mixed it in with the hot chocolate and set it down. My mother must have known from my face that something was up. This woman had a beautiful white suit on and my mother said, 'Mrs. Calkins, I wouldn't drink that if I were you. I don't like the look on my daughter's face.' And the welfare lady said, 'Oh, she's the loveliest girl, Marie.' So she took a sip and promptly spit it up."

When Jane was about six, her mother became completely bedridden as a result of an acute arthritic condition. It then became Jane's responsibility to take care of her, which included cooking, cleaning, bringing her the bedpan, and getting up in the middle of the night to refuel the stove. Her mother used to tell Jane that she was going to turn on the gas jets in the middle of the night and kill them both. "My mother was a real bitch," Jane says, "but she was an energetic bitch. When my mother attempted suicide for about the fifth time, she took a whole mess of sleeping pills and was in the hospital. I went to the welfare lady and said, I can't take it anymore. I've just got to leave."

Jane had been going with a fellow named Walter at the time, and they decided to go to the west coast by motorcycle to see Jane's father. Walt and Jane then married. "Three years we lived together," Jane says in an interview. "Then I found out—while I was working in a radio factory putting lover-boy Walt through school, everybody else in town knew—he isn't going through school." Then, Jane met Rob:

"I wrote him a poem the second time I met him. The fourth time, it was a party, we'd never kissed, we'd never had a date. I just looked at him and said, 'Look, I'm leaving Walt, and I'm going to leave by myself or I'm going to leave with you, so just let me know.'"

The following excerpt from one of Jane's personal journals, written in 1978, sheds some light on the nature of her relationship with Rob:

"I think, this minute anyhow, that I am lonely; except for Rob, my work or Seth's is so often misunderstood; used for ends that to me are unfortunate, as if somehow despite all Seth says or I say, we are just a slightly more exotic species of the psychic master and his holy sister." This passage reminded me of times when Jane questioned whether her books were really helping anyone, including those of us in class.

Over the years, hundreds of people witnessed Seth speaking. Some went to class for an evening, others attended for longer periods of time. Outside of the class structure, Jane gave many personal Seth sessions to various individuals who had written her asking for help. She never charged for those personal sessions. She did, however, charge $3.50 a class when I first attended. But when the Seth books began to sell in sufficient numbers, she dropped the fee.

During class, Jane remained seated in her rocking chair, as the vocal power of Seth and the Sumari seemed to shake the walls at times. About halfway through class, there was always a break when Jane would go across the hall to her other apartment for a short time, and then come back and resume class.

I remember a particular evening when Jane got up from her rocker to walk across the hall as I had seen her do so many times before, and yet this one night, it was as if I were watching her do this for the first time. I had never noticed the extreme difficulty she had in getting her legs to move, in just putting one foot in front of the other. It was an impression that never left me.

On the other side of the coin, the agility and flexibility of Jane's mental gymnastics were at times remarkable. The following episode occurred one night after class had officially ended for the evening.

Jane said, "Rich, look at me: now I am Jane." In that moment she was Jane as I knew her in her usual state. Then she closed her eyes for an instant, opened them, and said, "Now I am Sumari." Jane's face now displayed the look and feel of when she sang Sumari, a distinct difference from her usual countenance. Then, closing her eyes again and quickly opening them, she said in her normal voice, "Now I am what you think of as Seth, without the voice." I stared with wonder into Seth's eyes as he peered back into mine. Once again Jane closed her eyes, opened them, and Seth said, "Now I am what you think of as Seth with the voice!" Jane closed and opened her eyes again: "Now I am something you don't know yet." Eyes closed, opened, and she was back to the usual Jane, who then said, "Do you see the difference?"

I had just witnessed a demonstration in the nature of consciousness that lasted all of 30 seconds, a demonstration one could ponder for a lifetime.

Another incident from class that stands out in my mind transpired while Jane was singing Sumari. Due to Jane's arthritis, she was normally unable to lift her arm over her shoulder, yet one night while in trance singing Sumari, she lifted her arm high above her head to everyone's amazement.

When she came out of trance, the class informed her of what she had done, and she said that Seth had told her many times that there was nothing wrong with her bones. But now, no longer in trance Jane could barely lift her arm to shoulder level.

Another evening, when class had "officially" ended, Jane looked at Bobby Axelrod, one of the students, and spontaneously gave him the following reincarnational data: She told Bobby that he was a beautiful woman with long black hair with combs in it, and that he lived near Majorca, Spain. He was a highly skilled dancer, and had 8 children of which 5 were stillborn. He believed in a superstition at the time, that if a stillborn child was buried in the earth, the next would survive. Jane then said that in dancing and acting in this life, he has the ability to easily switch between male and female movements. So not only were we on the edge of our psychic chairs not knowing what Seth might say at any given moment, we also never knew what Jane might come up with:

"Rich, you were an Indian," Jane once commented to me, then just continued with class. Seemingly apropos of nothing, she looked at one of the students one evening and said, "I think you once killed me, yet not from hate, but clumsily. It almost seems amusing."

Another time she told that same student that at 14 years old he had picked up an idea about the nature of reality that has held him back sexually. She said a math course and a woman named Sylvia were involved. The student then revealed that in 10th grade Geometry, he had a teacher whose first name was Sylvia. These are just a few instances of what were no doubt thousands of psychic impressions Jane had during her lifetime.

In 1975 Jane and Rob bought a house which they referred to as "The Hill House." When Jane continued classes at their new home she was much more open than she had been before.

I remember her talking about some person in class who, in her words, "used to drive me up a wall." Listening to her speak like that surprised me. I guess I was so mesmerized by Seth and so struck by Jane's abilities, that evidence from Jane of the everyday feelings we all have caught me off guard. One note along these lines: Jane once told us that if she wanted to, she could have had us all wrapped around her finger, but it was an important point in her development not to use her abilities in such a manner.

People came to Jane always wanting something, and add to that the fact that they rarely ever wanted that something from Jane, but from Seth. Jane mentioned once that she still resented it when new people came to class with the attitude "will Seth come through?"

The Air Force once contacted Jane to see if she could help locate a missing pilot whose plane had crashed while he was on a training mission in upstate New York. Jane told them she had an impression of the letter M and Twin Mountains, and the pilot was found at Mt. Matumbel. She then picked up so much about the pilot that the government became suspicious that she may have somehow been involved in the whole incident; an interesting example of what can happen when unofficial abilities meet the official world.

The following passage from one of Jane's personal journals caught my eye recently: "I dreamed that in the future, all households would be connected to interconnecting computers, keeping track of all inhabitants, actions, goods, and so forth." This was written in 1981, long before the word Internet and personal computers were a part of our everyday lives. Jane, by the way, never used a computer, said she hated typing her own material, and admitted to being a lousy speller.

The following incident also occurred in 1981, and once again underscores the great depth of Jane's abilities. I was experiencing some health problems, which led me to call Jane. I was not able to speak with her, but spoke briefly with Rob, who said he would relay my message.

I then took the train to the city to run some errands, and while walking around Manhattan, I felt a sudden wave of calm energy encircling my entire body. It was quite tangible. I didn't connect the experience with my phone call to Jane, since I had not spoken with her.

I returned home about 7:00 p.m. and Jane called. She told me she had tried to reach me by phone numerous times during the afternoon, and when unsuccessful, she concentrated on sending me energy, imagining it all over my body. She then went on to discuss some of the reasons she was picking up that were behind my health problems.

The following is a paraphrase of Jane's comments to me:

> You have a characteristic of being very expressive with your energy, and then clamping down on it by tightening your muscles, which are a part of your health problems. Don't be afraid of this characteristic, but be aware that when you feel panicky, you are not using your energy easily.
>
> Your health problems are also, of course, connected to your life situation, and your current relationship also plays a part in this. Also realize that taking care of yourself is as natural as the social situation, and don't let your age make you ashamed of working in whatever job you have, be it at a factory or whatever.

She went on to say that our society is based on the idea that everything that can go wrong will, and that I should tell myself that things will work out in their own way. Jane then said she "got" the following exercise for me to try: "Imagine a small doll in your image, a smaller version of you, and talk to it, tell it everything will be okay. Tell it that it is a good doll; that you will protect it, and give yourself a break and love it."

It was only years later that I realized the extent of Jane's own health problems at that time, and yet she was able to reach out with healing energy for others.

I'm going to end with an excerpt from one of Jane's personal journals, written three years before her death:

> Sometimes, I think that we're just like slaves, afraid to be free. We yell, rattle our chains, yet are consoled by the sounds they make. And if one breaks, we forge new links and repair it in the secret dark, then piteously hold out our sore hands to demonstrate our misery. If we form our own realities, then surely a knowledge of that fact must fill us with self-reproach when we view those areas of experience in which deficiencies are only too apparent. The question is, why do we create thorns so often in place of flowers and then bemoan our fates, or blame ourselves in agonies of self-defeat?
>
> For one thing, we've been taught and believe that illness, for example, is negative, bad, and destructive. So how do we regard poor health when we no longer assign its source to infection, viruses, gods or demons, or to life's strange vagaries? If we realize finally that we form our own prisons, why do we stubbornly still insist upon doing so?

Jane Roberts Collage

Presented by me at the 1997 Seth Conference in Elmira, NY.

In trying to put together a collage of Jane, I started out feeling a bit overwhelmed. Jane's creative output was so vast and so exceptional, how does one choose what to present? With the conference quickly approaching, I was feeling pressured, but still didn't have a handle on how to proceed. And then, out of the blue, I heard a little voice say: "Did you ever think of just being playful?" Playful? I had forgotten about that one. So I took the advice to heart and proceeded to choose a variety of excerpts from Jane's letters, poems, personal journals, conversations, and interviews, both before and after the emergence of Seth. I also decided to let the excerpts find their own order rather than trying to arrange them chronologically. So now let's hear what Jane has to say.

Am married, no children, but a terrific cat named William Loehman Butts. Husband is an artist. He designs labels in a local plant four hours a day (in the art department), and the other four he paints, writes, or sometimes when we need more cash, does commercial work. Yours truly, with an old bicycle and three baskets, wearing slacks, oodles of sweaters, and bright lipstick, sells Avon products three hours a day, and between us, financially, we manage pretty well. This includes rent on our three rooms (five rooms now), Rob made me two rooms out of the attic. They are cardboard rooms with cardboard walls, but well insulated, and covered with paintings, our daily supply of food, cigarettes, magazines and books. Our apartment, our work, and our love is our life.

Sunday—A beautiful day! We went dancing last night as usual and had a great time. Today we have to drive down to see Rob's dad in Troy at the home. I cleaned the house up. Rob is painting. Len downstairs, just back from vacation, is mowing the grass. I realize how lucky I am, how great our lives are, Rob's and mine, compared to tragedies of others. If I had a rough time in early years, certainly not now. Why was I so complaining and unable to emotionally enjoy life for a while? What joy each day, and how we so often project all kinds of restrictions upon our own subjective enjoyment.

A gigantic thunderstorm begins around suppertime. We eat watching *Star Trek*, and Rob goes down to the basement to see if there's water there. Suddenly, I'm aware that my right hand closes easily, without resistance; sometimes it closes now and then, but always with resistance. I clean up the kitchen while the storm rages. Once, lightning strikes close or so it seems; a snapping sound and flash of white; my knees tremble and go woozy. Now I sit at the table, elbow and right arm working better; and right toes feel woozy. It's humid, still pouring rain. And for a moment, the oddest sensation—as if the inner and outer conditions merge completely. The stormy landscape, a perfect counterpart of my inside world. The thunder rolling around the hills—MY angers rousing and releasing themselves; the teeming rain, my own frustrations and tears released in a torrent over inner landscapes. No wonder my hand suddenly freed; old stubbornnesses rolling off my shoulders; a cool refreshing wind still angry, but clear, blowing through my skull. The feeling was amazingly fleet, but complete. I was exhilarated by the storm, and I felt like driving in the rain down to the corner, to see how much water had collected at the intersection, or even like making noise, singing or something.

All of a sudden, with no transition at all, I left my body. My consciousness just flew right out over Water Street. There was a nail in the window and, shit, I can't explain it, but as I went out I sort of merged with the nail, and flowed through the leaves of the pear tree, and flowed through the bark, and I knew that everything had life—that the nail was alive; that the atoms and the molecules in it had a consciousness; that the world was amazingly alive no matter how dead anything looked. The next thing, I was back in my body and my note pad, which had been there for writing poetry, was full of writing that I must have done while I'd been out of body. It was called, "The Physical Universe As Idea Construction."

The Seth Material is my unique source and a literally fabulous one that I really did not truly appreciate, and to which I was not really directed. It is as if clouds of the worst sort have rolled away. Rereading some material, I was struck by the massive intellect behind it, the real beauty of the material, and sad that I did not really let myself realize it before; indeed, that I had allowed myself to be affected by the lesser writings of others; even to the extent that in some late sessions it affected the material. I feared setting myself up as some sort of a false prophet. I could go on television, and make a lot of money, but it would take away from other more important things to me, and the rich personal relationships I have in class. Class is as far as I'll go besides the books. Whatever Seth has to offer, it's in very personal terms, and the same for me. I am not going to be a Seth missionary for mass audiences.

Took a bath, had fun bathing, perfuming, yet felt to some degree I should be working. But doing nothing may be good for both of us, like when I sit at the table after dinner watching trees. Sometimes I justify it by saying I get poetry ideas, which I do, but I think now I realize doing this is good—because it feels good—and puts me in touch with myself and nature. Most important: do what I want to do first, not what I think I ought to do. I am free to do what I want; pursue the psychic work or not, what parts of it I want, not do others, get a job, volunteer work, go outside, do Christmas shopping. I am free to do whatever I want, how come I thought I wasn't?

Anyone getting really good material and giving it out publicly is in a position of proving that it's true in a physical fact relationship, and any proofs automatically water down the material, making it less valid and forcing it into a lesser context. Hence, the spirit guide bit. You will be put in the position where you have to tell the public, yes, this is a spirit, and he's really alive and all this stuff. Or, I'm a fraud, or a schizoid.

I was regarded as having the truth and a spirit guide, and I'm speaking generally here, by spiritualists and those in the field, or being a fraud or psychologically disturbed at the other end, and in that frame of reference there is no in-between. Either I was looked up to, not as myself, but because of Seth, or I was thought of as a nut and disturbed. And I refused the entire framework. It denied me my own joy and contact in a way I can't explain. Spirit guide terminology is completely inaccurate to explain personalities such as Seth, and any of the same kind that you might encounter as a result of your own experience. I do not believe they are spirits in the terms meant. I consider the Seth material as evidence of other Aspects of the multidimensional personality.

The person I am in my time can really get screwed up trying to figure out in what terms Seth is or isn't valid, or what he is. Would a Seth, experiencing Jane, think of her as a lesser developed personality? Maybe, but just maybe, he'd also think of her as one with great growing potential to be encouraged, so that in time terms, he with his ability could emerge. He would be me, in my present time, developing abilities that would later let him be him. And simultaneously, I would be developed. And simultaneously I would be him developing and guiding me in my present time. The usual spirit interpretation isn't a step ahead of the normal psychological explanation at all, because they automatically take it for granted that the guide is outside ourselves or independent, because inside or coexistent sounds awful and means it's just you, and you know you're nothing.

The symptoms are a constant reminder to be more understanding of others. If I were completely healthy I'd be apt to be more impatient with others. The symptoms help me relate to others' problems in a way I wouldn't otherwise. Keeping them as a reminder, no one, including myself, is perfect, to keep me from getting a big head, from going off half-cocked. So after good news I emphasize the symptoms, so I don't feel superior.

I sit at the typewriter and through the window I see a fantastic autumn day and revel in it. The sudden clearness right now of suddenly visible sky that was until lately filled with leaves; yet I feel my anxiety strongly. Annoyed by kitten who is playing with paper on floor and anger goes out toward the kitten, but realize the anger is independent of the kitten and think the kitten represents something. The compulsive need to take care of something who needs care as mother did; the resentment at having to do so. My 'helplessness' is a power play. Try to put it clearly. No way to defend self against mother as a kid, forced to care for her yet felt she had no use for me for doing it; if I had gumption I wouldn't; she detested me. So I had this great anxiety.

With the psychic stuff, suddenly others started looking to me for help. All of this was hatred against mother, being forced to help her, I wouldn't do it again; so when the situation arose, I looked helpless so people would see I couldn't help them when I couldn't help myself. Only way I could express hostility safely against mother, or against other people who had something wrong and wanted help. You couldn't yell at them or do anything; by their need, they controlled you.

If I hurt, too, they won't see what I'm doing and neither will I. So don't have to take the responsibility of refusing to help. At same time, idea of being powerful, the greatest, is a way of getting back and defending self. So get these abilities then refuse to use them—brings sense of power. The anxiety became a force again when I was needed to help. Not succeeding all the way, also of getting back at her—all ways of releasing hostility; only way that seemed open. Anyone could be cast in the old mother stance, Rob too; so my 'helplessness' makes him do things for me: power play, I control him through symptoms as my mother did me! Cut off nose to spite face.

Can release these feelings creatively through writing now, and conscious awareness should help. Sense of power and expression of hostility in not acting as I'm supposed to; not using psychic abilities fully, not functioning as I should, prevents me from taking joy in real achievements. If I realize I'm OK, as good as anyone else, if Rob can help me by loving me lots and I keep this stuff in mind, I can make it."

I was sitting in the yard the other day working on *Psychic Politics*, and I'm getting some great ideas and there's a whole bunch I didn't bother writing down. I was watching a dog, we had a dead rabbit out there, and the dog was going wild rolling on the dead rabbit, and for some reason I translated that as rolling in shit. And I was thinking, we think that is so terrible, if we let go, what are we going to do, we might do something awful like have an orgasm rolling in shit, or that it would be so awful and so primitive and so uncivilized and so unspiritual, that that's what we'd do.

And I was thinking, how crazy. For centuries we've gone to war, and we think that is a heroic manly act worthy of a human being. Almost any man I think, would rather be caught, even with a gun in his hands in the face of his enemy shooting him to death, than rolling in shit laughing his head off, out in the backyard.

I still resent it when new people come to class with the attitude—will Seth come through? If you're waiting for me to have Seth come through, you should be as anxious to hear your own inner selves come through. You look for wonders from me, when you should look for wonders from yourselves. And there are wonders; you think there aren't any, there's all kinds of wonders from yourselves.

You have all kinds of potentialities right now, not that you necessarily have to wait for or work for or anything, but that you have now. And when you look at me and want Seth to come through, and when you don't want to know what Jane says, but you want to know what Seth says, you are denying your own reality. You are denying your own inner voice. Because you're saying, well, Jane is just an individual, and she can't know, but Seth knows, and I'm an individual, and I don't know, but Seth knows. But without me Seth couldn't speak, and without your inner selves, you wouldn't have the knowledge.

All I want you to do, is if you hear your own voice, not to distrust it. Why, because it's somebody else's voice, does it all of a sudden attain authenticity, where your own voice doesn't? You distrust your own experience, and for some odd reason trust other people's, and this is what I want you to get away from.

I'm not wrong often, but when I'm wrong, I'll tell you, and I was wrong. Comet does work better than Ajax. For years I have used Ajax, and I watched this commercial about the New York sinks and I was down at 458 Water Street and I used Ajax, and while my sink was still sort of black at the bottom, it got the crap up.

We moved into our new house and I moved into a house with an immaculate goddamn sink. I looked at it and it was absolutely immaculate, and I started cleaning it with my Ajax. It got dirtier and dirtier and dirtier. And I was scrubbing and scrubbing and scrubbing. One night, Rob and I were sitting here, when the revelation came, and on television there was this commercial, and it said, "Comet works better than Ajax." Now I figured "A" came first in the alphabet so Ajax had to work better, right? The next time we went shopping—I bought a can of Comet. And all the stains came off my sink. They really did.

Francois, Cults and Breaking Free

In chapter 11 of my book, *The Road To Elmira*, I discuss the class where Seth spoke about Francois, a metaphysical teacher I had followed for about two years. In this piece I share in greater detail the events behind my joining Francois' group, and the events which led to my breaking away from Francois and the cult he had established.

In 1969, along with many of my friends, I began studying philosophy under a man named Francois Nesbitte. Larry Herschaft, a friend, was the first person to learn of Francois, from an ad Francois had posted in a local paper. Francois described himself as a spiritual master, claiming to have achieved levels of enlightenment that few had attained. He called his system of philosophy, "The Gnosis," stating that his extensive knowledge of the universe came from secret or esoteric teachings.

Francois had a number of students, and his goal, once those students were sufficiently trained, was to open a school where they would spread his teachings to "the masses," so as to save mankind from extinction. And although his students were growing in number, only a select few would be allowed to officially become part of his school, while others would not. I was in the "not" category.

The "chosen few" that Francois did deem worthy, were encouraged to take up residence in the same place, in this case a hotel in Manhattan called Hayden Hall. These folks were further instructed to not mingle with those whom he had decided were not to be among the "chosen." For all intents and purposes, The Gnosis was a cult, with Francois as the leader. Through his actions and his words, Francois divided us, pitted us against each other, and put a strain on many long-term friendships.

Francois also designated a series of books that each of the students were to purchase, and these books were to be read in a specific order as determined by Francois. He would also decide when each student could move on to the next book in the series.

In late 1970, Francois added the book, *The Seth Material* to his required reading list. He told us that Seth was very advanced spiritually, but that Jane was messed up, and that she controlled Rob. We later found out that Francois had spoken with Jane a number of times over the phone, insisting their teachings and goals were the same, an assessment Jane strongly disagreed with. Later on Jane told us that Francois used to "drive her up a wall."

In the summer of 1971 I wrote Jane a letter asking if I could attend one of Jane's classes, not mentioning my affiliation with Francois. She wrote back saying I could come up anytime, but to let her know beforehand.

Jeff Marcus, a friend of mine, who like me was excluded from Francois' school, decided he also wanted to attend one of Jane's classes, and asked Francois for permission to do so. Francois told him by all means to go, if Jane allowed it.

On September 20, 1971, Jeff got a lift to Ithaca, NY, and the next day he hitched from Ithaca to Elmira to attend Jane's September 21, 1971 class. He didn't call Jane beforehand, but she let him attend. Jeff had to go to work the next day, so he left class after the first hour and a half and took the bus back to New York City. As a result, Jeff was not there when Seth came through, because Seth came through later in the evening. For the hour or so Jeff did attend, class had revolved around a fellow named Wilson Brinker, an older man from Pennsylvania, who is called Martin Crocker in Sue Watkins' book, *Conversations With Seth*.

A few months after Jeff attended this class, specifically during the last week of December 1971, Francois suddenly died. It seemed impossible that someone so charismatic and filled with energy could suddenly just drop dead on the streets of Manhattan one afternoon, but that was what happened.

To say the least, his death greatly affected all of us who were followers of Francois, leaving many of us unsure now how to proceed with our lives. The death of Francois ended up serving as a strong impetus for us to contact Jane again.

Jeff was the one who called Jane to tell her that Francois had died, to which she replied that someone had already let her know. During that phone call he also asked Jane if a few of us could attend one of her classes, to which she agreed. So on January 4, 1972, approximately one week after the death of Francois, we went up to Elmira by car, and attended what turned out to be our first ESP Class.

Fast forward to the first week of October in 1972. We had been attending Jane's classes for approximately ten months now, and during that time had become friends with Sue Watkins. The next class was scheduled for

October 10, and we decided to go up a few days early to visit with Sue. Sue's apartment was on Water Street, just a few blocks from where Jane lived and held her classes.

On the way up to Sue's, I had an anxiety attack, and at one point it got so bad I told Jeff he should just drop me off by the side of the road and I would hitch back to New York City. Jeff was able to finally calm me down. And Jeff was not at his best either, dealing with a bad sore throat that wasn't getting any better. On some level we definitely sensed the events that were soon to transpire during the upcoming class.

While staying with Sue, Jeff and I spoke of how amazing Francois was (despite the fact he had been dead for almost a year.) It was obvious to Sue that we were still under Francois' spell. Unbeknownst to us, Sue mentioned this fact to Jane, thereby playing a significant role in Seth finally speaking out about Francois and his teachings during the class of October 10, 1972.

Here are some of the comments made by Seth during that class pertaining to Francois and his teachings:

> And woe to the man or woman who is the weight, who bears the weight, of heavy tribute for such a one is no longer free. And so I take tribute and throw it out the window like a child's ball, and let it fly where it may, or I play with it! For those who offer you tribute, offer you also the weight of their own responsibility. The one who accepts such tribute do not understand what they are doing. And I always understand what I am doing.
>
> He who lords it over others makes himself into a false god. And he who drinks with gluttony the tribute of others, needs it worse than drugs. And he who confuses you, confuses himself. And he who speaks to you in ambiguous terms does so because he does not see clearly.
>
> The man who says, or the spirit who says, "I alone have the truth and these are the maps and this is the only way," or implies it through his teachings or his actions, does not have the way. The man or the spirit who sets himself up above you is not above you. There is no above or below in those terms. Each consciousness has its own meaning and

its own integrity and its own beauty, as you have yours (to Rich), and you have yours (to Jeff).

Any man who tells you, "This knowledge is secret and I will only tell it to the violets or the roses or the clouds or the seagulls," does not have the knowledge. It is free as the air that flows inconspicuously through your cosmic cheeks. It belongs to you. He who sets up closets of secrecy (to Rich) has nothing worth hiding.

There is nothing for which you need feel guilty. As Ruburt would say, "Do not make a big deal of it!" That kind of responsibility is not yours anymore than it was Francois'. The responsibility is within each individual and within each of the members of the group. You cannot try to shoulder it for them, or you fall into the same trap. Now here there is no trap. There is only freedom. I am not being ambiguous, and if you hoped I would speak out I am doing so.

To Rich: "It was not a reprimand. Nor was I putting your friend down, but explaining the state of his experience and the pitfalls into which he fell."

Rich: "Was that pitfall materialized physically also?"

Seth: "Of course it was. They always are."

Seth: "He well knew what would happen when he acquiesced to you coming here, and he did that for you. And do not forget it."

(Rich surmised that if he was able to assimilate what Seth had said he might be able to "re-enter the human race.")

Seth: "You never left it. But I should hardly be the one to tell you that!"

The following letter that I wrote to Jane represents the first contact I had with her. It is a request by me to attend one of Jane's classes. Reading it now, it's rather embarrassing, but at the time, that's where I was at.

[1971 Jun?]

Dear Jane and Rob,

I live in New York City, am twenty years old, and my name is Richard Nissenbaum. I am studying and living philosophy so as to bring into actuality the infinity of all that I am. I have studied and continue to study books by Carl Jung; such as Mysterium Coniunctionis, Aion, Psychology and Alchemy, as well as books by many who far exceeded the knowledge and understanding of Jung.

I would like to know if it would be possible to visit you for even an hour or two to read some of the other Seth material you have, and of course if possible, attend a session. The access to some of the knowledge in your unprinted material alone would satisfy me greatly. If neither is possible, I would appreciate it if you could find the time to at least send me a postcard, telling me when to expect the next book. Your respectful initiate:

Richard Nissenbaum
150-20-71 AVE
Kew Garden Hills,
N.Y.C. N.Y.

Marguerite de Valois

[As detailed in chapter 8 of my book, *The Road To Elmira*, Marguerite de Valois represents one of my reincarnational selves. The following incident occurred in 2012 and shows how connections with "past" selves continue to exist in our current lives.]

In May of 2012, a Seth reader from The Netherlands who I had exchanged some messages on Facebook with had come to Connecticut to attend a wedding. She was staying in New Haven (where I live), so we got together one evening and had a fun time discussing the Seth material. During the evening, for some reason Marguerite de Valois kept coming to mind, and I felt a strong impulse to share some pictures I had of Marguerite with my Netherlands visitor, and since my apartment was only a short distance from where she was staying, I went home and retrieved the pictures.

She mentioned during the evening that tomorrow she was planning to take the train into New York City, where there were a number of places she wanted to visit. One of those places was the Frick Museum, where there was a Renoir exhibit that was taking place. Though I don't know much about Renoir, I impulsively asked if I could join her during her visit to the museum, and she said yes.

Marguerite de Valois as a child

As I walked into the room containing the Renoir paintings, the very first picture I looked at really bothered me, though I had no idea why. I had such a negative reaction to it that I decided I wouldn't read the plaque below the picture, which gave background information about the painting, which I would normally always be curious to read.

The room contained only nine pictures by Renoir, and after viewing all of them, and reading the notes that accompanied them, I decided before we left I might as well review that first one to which I had such a negative reaction to. The title was "Madame

Henriot en travesti" (The Page). Here is the information on the plaque that accompanied the painting:

> Renoir's eighteen-year-old model, Marie-Henriette Grossin — an actress who later adopted the stage name Madame Henriot — appears before a red velvet curtain, with a glimpse of the theater behind her. She is playing a boy's role, as we can see from her costume, and wears a long-sleeved doublet with buttons fastened tightly down the center, reminiscent of a troubadour. Eager to make his mark as a painter of theatrical celebrities, Renoir may have posed Henriot as the beautiful page Urbain, who serves Queen Marguerite de Valois in "Les Huguenots," an immensely popular opera set in the sixteenth century.

After seeing the name Marguerite de Valois my consciousness just came to an abrupt stop. I've had this kind or reaction before when reality seems to turn sideways as certain kinds of data presents itself. When I regained my mental composure, I thought about the night before, and how I had felt Marguerite's presence on and off throughout the evening.

My negative reaction to that Renoir painting made me wonder if I was picking up Marguerite's feelings regarding a page that had served her in sixteenth century France.

I believe the connections between selves are always near, making themselves known to us in a variety of ways. Sometimes they are waving to us through three-dimensional windows in the clear

Marguerite de Valois as a young woman

light of day; other times they are discreetly peeking out from behind lace-colored curtains from dusty rooms in long-forgotten castles; and there are moments they seem to be whistling in the wind, though we attribute the unknown sounds to the wind just playing tricks on us.

If it *is* just the wind playing tricks on us, what miraculous breezes blow through the centuries, carrying strands of consciousness that go unnoticed as they seamlessly weave in and out of our daily lives? But each time we do become aware of their presence, the illusions of time and space fall away, revealing a picture that straddles both past and future, creating a timeless now, in our present.

SNAPSHOTS IN TIME

❖ ❖ ❖

The Shit Hit the Fan

I'd smoke pot for the first time, and leave behind dreams of playing third base for the New York Yankees.

I'd turn my back on organized religion as I felt it had turned its back on me.

The television shows that used to keep me glued to the TV set every Friday night would give way to real life dramas where Father DID NOT Know Best, and I'd Dream of Jeannie in ways I never would have done a few years earlier.

I would start going to Greenwich Village, where I would discover a counter-culture that would soon clash with the culture that had been put in place by the former generation, and which I had up until then unquestioningly accepted.

My hair would soon reach my shoulders to the great alarm of my parents, as I was physically dragged one day to the barber for a crew-cut, as if that somehow could forestall the changes that we all knew would shortly be upon us.

This picture of me was taken right around the time the shit was about to hit the fan.

Authority figures of my youth would turn into Mickey Mouse, as going to Disneyland was no longer a priority on my wish list.

As I waited tables at The Bottom Line (one of the hippest jazz clubs in New York City at the time), the sounds of a new generation's music would fill my head with images and sensations that Sinatra and Count Basie, as great as they were, just couldn't compete with.

"Negroes" would turn into "Blacks" (only later to change into "African Americans") and when I was seen by a neighbor bringing one of "them" into my house, the event created such an uproar that one might have thought we were on the brink of WWIII.

In the little enclave of garden apartments I lived in it would soon become common knowledge that this woman who had seemed to have the perfect marriage had instead engaged in an affair with one of the neighborhood men, who also seemed to be a paragon of virtue. The scandal that ensued was of mega-proportions and every time this woman walked by she was followed by whispers and snickering. (Note that the man was not subject to the same kind of treatment.)

But all of this was nothing compared to the time when one of the young men who lived nearby was found out to be gay. The response to that was too terrible to include even in a book like this.

Money and Western medicine were soon to become our new Gods, and young men from all kinds of backgrounds would be sent to a land thousands of miles away to wage a war that we later found out was based on lies and deceit.

Flags were burned, bras were burned, cities were burned, and when the smoke cleared, the picture that emerged of the country I grew up in was far different than that which was presented to me in school.

The shit did indeed hit the fan shortly after this picture was taken, but perhaps that's the way it is with each new generation.

Old myths die and new ones are born; the heroes of the past become the villains of the future; the oppressed become the oppressors, and so it goes, until perhaps one day a world vision appears so bright, so imbued with truth and beauty, that it serves as an ideal for many generations to come. Until inevitably, the shit hits the fan once again.

Junior High School 194

As I look at this picture of myself in Junior High School (middle row, center) there is something about the way the lips curl ever so slightly that looks almost like a smirk, and hints of a certain disdain for conventional things, including probably the fact that I had to have my picture taken in the first place.

I'm pretty sure I must have resented being forced to wear a tie for this picture, for ties are something I have always disliked. I've never understood

WM   H   CARR
J H S   194   QUEENS
CLASS   9-304
1964-65

the reason why people wear ties. Why would someone want to take a piece of cloth, tie it into a knot, and then squeeze it around their neck and have it remain there for the entire day? One of the first things people do when coming home from work is to take their ties off so as to feel more comfortable. So why put the damn thing on to begin with?

Perhaps wearing a tie symbolizes one's willingness to take orders from others, to follow rules whether one agrees with them or not. I also suspect that some people feel that by wearing a tie their stature and worth is somehow automatically elevated (like wearing a uniform).

Who the hell invented ties anyway? Probably the same person that came up with using starch in shirt collars. But enough about ties for the moment.

Let's move on to my hair. This picture of me does not do justice to the pompadour I sported at the time, for it wasn't your typical pompadour. It wasn't your typical pompadour due to the fact that its ability to defy gravity was contrary to commonly accepted scientific principles that would have dictated otherwise.

My pompadour stood high up from my forehead and remained at exactly the same gravity-defying angle throughout the day. It was a perfect reflection of my stubborn nature, and I really believe that it was this stubbornness that was behind my pompadour's ability to maintain its position in space without any outside assistance, such as that which might come from a gel, or spray, or mousse.

Other aspects of this picture that stand out have to do with my shirt and vest. Most of the guys in the picture wore white shirts, while a few others (myself included) wore darker colored shirts. And while I was the only one to wear a vest, there was one other fellow (first row, second in from left) who was the only one to wear a sport jacket. As to this other fellow, his name was Richie Notarbartolo.

I haven't seen Richie since the 1960s when we hung out every now and then. I did however contact him last year (on Facebook). I had been thinking about old friends from the neighborhood and decided to see which ones might be listed on Facebook. When I came across Richie's name I also checked out his "Friends" and one of the names I came across was Lenora Bono. Her name caught my attention for two reasons. The first reason was that Lenora had a brother named John, and though he was a few years younger than me, we would often run into each other, and there was a really nice connection between us. Sadly, John died of a drug overdose at a very young age. But I will always remember his smile and the way we used to joke with one another.

The second reason Lenora's name caught my attention was that she was one of the first girls I ever kissed. There was this game we used to play at parties, something like spin the bottle, and because of the game I somehow ended up in the closet with Lenora for a few magical minutes.

So I searched for Lenora on Facebook, and when I saw she lived in New York City I sent her a friend request, but as of yet haven't heard anything back. (Perhaps I just wasn't a good enough kisser to warrant a response.)

Seth often spoke about alternate or probable realities, so perhaps there is an alternate reality, a parallel existence where John Bono did not die of a drug overdose, and Lenora and I got married and had lots of kids, and "Uncle"Richie Notarbartolo came over for Christmas and Easter, and life just ended up being a whole lot simpler than it is today. But whatever version of reality I find myself in, I'm still not going to wear a tie!

Bungalow Colony Memories

Summer in The Catskills,
A Walk On The Moon had not yet occurred,
But we were high on life,
As for me, I was a series of rocket explosions,
Energy bursting forth from sun-up to sundown.

I kissed a girl that summer,
My first kiss,
And the perfume of an older woman sent mind and body to
places I had never been to before.

Bungalow colony memories,
Swimming in the lake,
Toasting marshmallows by a glowing campfire,
And joyful anticipation stirring on even the cloudiest of days.

1950 Bungalow colonies,
Reduced today to so much scrap wood, used to heat the newly-
constructed McMansions now dotting the lake,
But no amount of renovation can erase those memories,
When the world was young,
And even my parents felt the joys of summer sun and winter
dreams.

My parents at a bungalow colony, circa 1958.

Jerry's Candy Store

Jerry's Candy Store-
Where hippy-dreams were born, later to be pummeled with Billy Clubs and tear gas on the streets of Chicago in 1968.

Jerry's Candy Store-
Where young men and women turned their backs on tradition, leaving in their wake hurt and angry parents, trying to control that which could no longer be controlled,

Jerry's Candy Store-
Where racing cars of the 1950s gave way to a different kind of speed, and psychedelic ice-cream sundaes danced on dusty counters,

Jerry's Candy Store-
Where the times were indeed a changin'—and the future was upon us before we had time to assimilate the present.

Jerry's Candy Store-
A microcosm of America in 1970,
Where the plastic coverings of the world began to fall apart,
And ugly truths long hidden began to show up in all their splendid tawdriness,

Jerry's Candy Store-
Where now sits a bank,
Such perfect symbolism as young men and women melted into society's main streets, disappearing seemingly overnight,

And Jerry, he took off in the middle of the night with all the candy, and stashed it in a vault of memories that I unlock every now and then with sweet nostalgia.

Rich Kendall, Jerry's Candy Store, circa 1969.

BITS AND PIECES

❖ ❖ ❖

Class Notes

The following comments are derived from notes I took during the time I attended Jane's classes.

Jane was talking about a 38 year-old woman in Elmira who was still a great belly dancer, and I made some comment about the woman's age and Jane said, Rich, you'll be in trouble with that belief.

One of the students in class said that Part Two of Jane's book, *Adventures In Consciousness*, sounded like a textbook, to which Jane replied that she hoped one day everything she wrote would be read as a textbook.

During class one evening Jane and Sue Watkins sensed the pyramid effect over Jane's head; Jane said Seth II was available to come through.

Jane once said she was picking up on Seth III.

Jane led the class in the following alteration of consciousness exercise:

> Accept the sounds. Don't think of the sounds as the sounds of cars. Experience the sound biologically. Experience the sound without looking for its origin. As you sit here, the sounds in ordinary terms will seem to come from outside the window. But as you hear them, simply accept them without looking for their origin. Then,

where do the sounds seem to be? You'll hear my voice. In ordinary terms my voice comes from me and I sit in a chair. Yet my voice is also a sound, and where does the sound come from? Don't ask, instead, accept the sound. What is inside, and what is outside? In certain terms your own reality belongs to both. I want you to even try to sense the air upon your skin, flowing through your skin. I'd like you to sense the floor, if you're sitting upon the floor; the chair or the couch, if you're sitting on a chair or the couch. I'd like you to sense in our terms, the greater reality of the chair or the floor or the couch. There is a greater reality behind objects. There's a greater reality behind the object of your own body, which is in this room in the same way that the chair or the couch or the table is in this room. I'd like you then to accept the full richness of your own experience in this moment. Now I would like you to try something else in whatever way you choose. I would like you though, if you can, imaginatively to follow me.

Don't worry where imagination begins or ends. Facts come from inner experiences. Life in many ways is a fiction we make real. Think of yourself as a little person leaving your head. Follow in whatever direction you feel like going. The joy and flexibility of letting your consciousness go in whatever direction it wants. Find a suspended period when you are free to travel. The moment can open up to other realities all packaged within this one.

Jane spoke of getting material too fast and too slow and the difficulty of trying to translate it neurologically into words through her physical mouth to our physical ears.

In one of her lives Jane was supposed to have been the artist, Van Dyke the Younger.

I mentioned in class one evening that I thought Sumari songs might also initiate dream experiences, and Jane told me that was pretty tricky and I was the first one to come up with that.

Jane speaking about Sumari during a class:

> When we try to get multidimensional experience through to your creaturehood, it has to come through your neurological structure. Somehow or other, what the Sumari is saying is that sound concentrates the experience so that you can physically perceive it. So that the sounds are concentrations of experience, and you'll have to clue me in on this later, because I don't know what the hell I'm talking about.
>
> When I do this particular kind of (trying to translate Sumari) I haven't learned quite how to do it yet because physically, I keep trying to pick this up and to know what the hell I've said, because I'm trying to get this so it makes some sense to people while I'm in both states at once.

Jane said with one mouth it's impossible to express what all the different Sumari channels are saying simultaneously as she is picking them up.

Sometimes in translating Sumari, Jane would say she was getting it both ways (Sumari and English at the same time.)

After singing Sumari one evening Jane came out of trance and exclaimed how beautiful the people in class looked, and how the colors she was seeing were beautiful.

While singing Sumari at times, they (through Jane) would look at individual class members and while singing to them mimic certain actions. One evening while Sumari was singing to me, they mimicked playing paddleball, first hitting the ball hard, and then soft. Another time they looked at me and made the motion of someone brushing their hair back.

One of the members of class was a music teacher and was speaking about how he would direct his students to maintain a certain posture while they were playing. Sumari came through with a song to him which Jane then translated:

> The translation is, the feelings sweep through the body, through these nerves and structures. Great music and emotion should sweep through the body, and then the body should move with emotion. And to tell them [the students] to sit upright is to inhibit not only the emotion that should sweep through the music, but inhibit the music that should flow freely with it through. And if you think you're doing a great thing by telling them to sit up straight, then you're cutting off the flow of the emotions, which will give the music its real vitality, and give you great music.

Jane sang the following in her usual Sumari trance, but did so in English, which was quite unusual:

> Follow your self
> The answers that spring up
> Like flowers that never bloomed
> The answers that spring up like
> Suns that never shone
> The lovers that never laid with you
> Follow the selves that are born
> Within your being now
> That sing within your dreams
> Now
> This self.

There was a Sumari song called "Jamala" after which Jane said, "If it's possible to go through five corners of a four cornered universe, I've done it."

Sumari came through with a song entitled "Soul Fossil Song." Jane said it was "a history of your being, being created now. This is my history and your history as Sumari. Everyone here tonight is Sumari. Being Sumari we seeded this earth with ourselves, that is, with our souls. We formed the bowels of the earth, the atoms and the molecules."

During class, Jane asked everyone to go around the room and spontaneously say something to each person. When I got to Jane I told her I felt I would have a stronger connection with her in death than in life. She didn't say anything but kissed me on the cheek.

Jane said to me one evening: "Rich, you are richly sane."

One of the members of class was talking about how his mother wanted him and his wife to have a baby, and Jane said, "Tell your mother if she wants to have a baby, let her have her own."

Before she died, Jane told Rob, "Don't let them make a god out of me."

Jane told someone in class that his eyes were like open roads.

Jane spoke of this guy who was shooting pigeons on the roof of a house next to where Jane lived, and she wondered why the pigeons kept coming back. The pigeons, she said, never took up arms and tried to shoot the man.

Jane said we are a species not pure beast or pure god, but perfect in our own way, though at times it was hard for her to see that.

There was a point not long before classes officially ended when a lot of new visitors came each week. This resulted in Seth covering much of the same ground we had been through many times already, and led us to feel a bit bored.

This got back to Jane, and Seth came through during a class saying that those who were bored need not feel obligated to come here anymore. I believe that the boredom we were beginning to feel was indicative of a point we had reached where it was time for us to get more involved with the world at large, and strive to incorporate Seth's ideas into that world. Jane said she didn't want people here who weren't here.

I was sitting in my kitchen one day feeling very frustrated that I didn't have a specific area in which to direct my energies. This was sometime in 1973. I told myself I was going to sit there until I made up my mind to choose some framework for my energy. I thought to myself at the time that I didn't want to write a book, though I enjoyed writing; and didn't want to become a musician though I enjoyed music. All of a sudden it hit me— writing lyrics expressing Seth's ideas through songs.

I then felt this tremendous rush of energy and called Jane. Before I got very far in my explanation she interrupted me and said, "Seth Rock, right?" She had instantly understood what I was trying to do.

A few months later I had a strong impulse to call Jane to update her regarding my efforts concerning "Seth Rock." She then informed me that sitting in her living room at that exact moment was Phoebe Snow, a singer and songwriter who was popular at the time. But more than that, Jane told me that moments before my call she was telling Phoebe Snow about my songs.

Tam Mossman, Jane's editor from Prentice Hall, was attending class one evening. I suddenly had the distinct feeling that he was a new probable self. I didn't mention this impression out loud, so was quite surprised when Jane and Sue Watkins mentioned the same thing as Tam Mossman was attempting to translate a Sumari song Jane had just sung.

Seth once told Jane he was glad she lived on such a nice street.

When class officially ended in 1975, a few of the students started getting involved in Scientology. Jane spoke of her conflicting reactions to this, saying that even though she always told us to do our own thing, this bothered her.

Lawrence Davidson, one of "The Boys From New York," who Jane was very fond of, had moved to Elmira for a while, but then decided to move to California. When he announced this one evening, Jane was obviously not pleased by this bit of news. She said to Lawrence, "Go ahead, go to California, eat your heart out, be free."

Nancy Borelli, a woman who had attended numerous classes, had a son who was five years old. She told class one evening that her son had just learned how to tie his shoes, yet he was playing classical music with remarkable proficiency. She also mentioned that since he was three years old he would see dancing triangles while in bed and would get scared. Seth told Nancy to tell her son the triangles were friendly.

Richard Kendall, um 1974

Rich Kendall in the living room of Jane Roberts during an ESP Class in 1974.

Jane said she used to get this skeleton feeling at times, and it scared her.

Rob said since the emergence of the Seth material, he was much less scared of growing older than he used to be.

Rob said he felt the whole human race, including himself, was just getting glimmerings into the nature of consciousness.

Sometime in the 1970s Jane "accidentally" set her blouse on fire in the kitchen. Rob ripped it off. She was scared and went into trance, gave herself suggestions, and hardly felt anything. She said she was aware she had been *stewing* about things.

Jane was talking about a television show she had been watching where a preacher was telling the viewers how their physical ailments could be healed through devoting themselves to Jesus Christ. Jane said even if she could be healed by following this method, she wouldn't do it.

In April 1976 I was talking to Jane about the possibility of my moving to Elmira, and Jane said there were no paddleball courts there, and that "game" wouldn't work up in Elmira. Jane was referring to the fact I was using all my energy playing paddleball, rather than dealing with basic issues in my life such as finding a job, and supporting myself. Here's a comment Seth made to me along those lines from an ESP Class dated August 6, 1974:

> I have a word for you – tonight, when you did not ask for my advice. Now, play paddleball with the universe. Play paddleball with the universe! In more mundane terms, in much more mundane terms, get out! Go into the world! Seek your own sustenance. You have the energy. You have the creativity. There is no job that you need fear, no contest before which you need to cower. You will not lose

your creativity in honest work, but find it, for it will add a new source to the creativity that is within you. But you need more feedback. And there is nothing that you need to fear. You are not a junior self. There is no need for you to put yourself in that position. You are not a kid – you are a young man. Then go with that young manhood out into the universe, and find yourself and the universe. Play paddleball with it.

And I tell you again, because I am such a grand old eccentric uncle, or because I allow myself to seem to be such a grand old eccentric uncle, that you can indeed triumph, and a 9 to 5 job is not going to destroy you – how fragile you must think that you are! What a trap you must consider it, that it would gobble your manhood and you could never escape!

I remarked one evening that Seth was "giving a good performance tonight" which prompted the following response: "It is not nearly as good as yours. I appreciate yours as much as you appreciate mine, but I understand mine, and yours, and you still do not understand your own!"

I once asked Jane what was happening in Elmira these days, and she said, "Everything."

One of the students, an older man who had never married and lived with his mother, was speaking of how he felt responsible for taking care of her.

Jane asked him why he would ever let himself be conned like that. Why would he think a woman would gobble him up any more than his mother had. And Jane asked him what he thought of women. She then said to me, "and that applies to you Rich!" Jane had told me a few years earlier that there was a probable reality that I would live with my parents the rest of my life.

(I did not live with my parents for the rest of my life, but I did live at home far longer than I should have. And when I hit a "bump in the road" at one point when I was in my fifties, finding myself with no job and no place to live, I went to live with my mother in Florida which lasted about nine months.)

I told Jane I saw eternity while on LSD and she said she did also, without any drugs. Jane said, if you want to get stoned, get stoned on timelessness.

I spoke of taking heroin to try to find peace, and Jane said she never searched for peace.

Jane had once saved a wounded bird from a cat and caused the bird three days of agony before it died. She realized afterward it would have been better to let the bird die naturally at the hands of the cat. Jane said the animals understand each other.

I told of a dream I had where I became conscious in the dream state and decided to try to find Seth. In commenting about the dream, Jane said to me, "Sometimes you have to grow older before you grow younger."

One of the students said for her to take the time to write down interpretations of her dreams she'd have to be writing for the rest of her life, and that would be silly. Jane responded by saying she didn't think that would be so silly.

Jane was talking about getting stuff from the Edgar Cayce Foundation and that they recommended numerous books, including every sappy psychic book as well as some excellent ones.

❖

Rich Kendall standing in front of 458 West Water Street, Elmira, NY. (1986)

Jane often felt free enough to just say "I don't know" in response to questions asked of her.

❖

The guys from New York City were talking during a class about starting a school in New York to teach the Seth Material, and to my surprise Jane didn't seem opposed to the idea, and said she thought we would do a good job.

❖

When Jane met Rob in 1953 she was still a virgin, though she had been previously married.

❖

Seth started speaking through Jane in 1963 when Jane was thirty four years old and Rob was forty four.

❖

Shortly after Jane and Rob met, Rob gave Jane a box of erasers that artists use. On one of the erasers Rob had written, "Make a galaxy, Jane." This was ten years before the Seth phenomenon began.

Jane was relating some incident where a woman told her about this guy who said the woman was beautiful, and Jane told her the guy said that to all the women, and the woman's face dropped. Jane then realized she shouldn't have said that because the woman needed that reinforcement.

Even though Jane and Rob had been together twenty years, Jane got wildly jealous while waiting for Rob to return after dropping a woman off at her motel who Jane had just held a private session for. The session had to do with this woman's problem with compulsive masturbation.

Jane was talking about some new development that occurred with the Seth material, and said if she knew how this was to be expanded in the next session she would have been a nervous wreck.

Jane often cautioned us about seeing people only in terms of their beliefs.

A guy called Jane and said a psychic told him he was a "Speaker." Jane responded by saying a daisy is a Speaker, and the caller didn't like that answer. (The "Speakers" are mentioned in Jane's fictional novel, *The Education Of Oversoul Seven*, as well as in various other places throughout the material.)

People used to call Jane on the phone and say they were Socrates, or Saint Paul, and one guy said he was both.

When people told Jane about staying home and experimenting with psychic experience, she would often ask them if they were working. She didn't feel it was beneficial for people to use psychic exploration as an excuse to avoid dealing with the world.

❖

Jane thought of Rooney, her cat, as her mother, and felt she had to take care of her, as she had felt about her mother. Rooney and Jane were not at ease with each other, and when Jane's mother died, there was no reason for the cat to stick around. When Jane buried the cat she was burying feelings about her mother.

❖

Jane once said during class, "I'm off, that's Ruburt." Then she said, "This is Jane."

❖

Speaking about going into trance, Jane said she jumps in in a funny fashion without questioning.

❖

Jane said that at times she would take the Seth energy and send it around the room.

❖

"Helper" for Jane was a pyramid with arms. (For information about Helper, see Jane's book *Adventures In Consciousness*.)

❖

Jane said she felt like Cypress (the character in Oversoul Seven) when doing the female Sumari voice.

Direct Quotes from Jane

- "We teach ourselves in ways that Seth or I could not."

- "We're so used to not trusting ourselves. We're taught anything is more dependable than we are."

- "Our food participates in our experiences in its own way."

- "There is an absolute terror behind the fear of aging when you believe the older you get the more degrading it becomes, and this fear and awareness of old age starts at about seventeen years old."

- "If at any time I felt powerless in regards to letting Seth come through I would have quit the whole thing. There were times I said No in regards to letting Seth come through."

- "Even those who seem to go along unquestioningly with it all, have their questions."

- "I choose to believe there is purpose and meaning to all, that we create our own reality, and that there is no in-between. If we came from cosmic dust then we will make meaning out of it."

- "Others would go batty with my life and vice versa. Every morning I wake up at 4:30 a.m. and write down my dreams. I don't even give myself the suggestion. I just do it. During one summer I worked from 2:00 a.m. to 7:00 a.m."

- "You can get so hung up on the ideal version of someone you love that you can forget the person in a certain way. I did that with Rob, worshipping him for many years; and to deal with someone in that way is not fair to them."

- "In a really funny way I feel the answers are reflected now in each moment, and by following them through we can learn about them."

♦   "Seth's ideas are the best road map I have yet found."

♦   "I had thought ouija boards were bullshit. I started the whole thing when Kennedy was killed and felt the country was going mad. I was really into politics at the time and writing poetry about Oswald, etc." (Lee Harvey Oswald was the man who assassinated President John. F. Kennedy in 1963.)

Front, L to R: Mary Rouen, Robert Butts, Susan Watkins, Mary Dillman
Back, L to R: Michael Steffen, Lynda Dahl, Rich Kendall. Picture taken in front of
"The Hill House," in Elmira, NY, during the 1999 Seth Conference.

♦   "I didn't know if these concepts about consciousness were true in late 1971, but I knew they were changing our consciousness."

♦   "Seth had said this guy Bill would come to class on a particular night and when he didn't, I got upset and thought since Seth was wrong about this, maybe I was distorting everything."

♦   "People think it is wrong to want to be great and say don't try to be great, settle for good."

♦   "We have new people in class so we don't get a closed cult where you can't stand hearing other people's beliefs, especially beliefs that differ from ours."

♦ "During some social gathering I was terrified to go into the backyard with the doctors' and lawyers' wives. They thought I was a snob when I was really just terrified. Earlier in my life I didn't look at people as individuals, but made social and economic divisions."

♦ "I once wrote a poem from a man's point of view about the joys of the penis."

♦ "I believe ideas are more powerful than anything else and are the only way to transform this world."

♦ "If you believe you are tainted from the start, then you need immunizations, shots, etc. to protect the 'fragile' body."

♦ "We think of the sun and planets as natural but put ourselves outside of nature, yet our thoughts are like tides."

♦ "I once told an insurance salesman I had insurance, rather than go into my beliefs about the whole thing."

♦ "There are still a lot of beliefs I am working on."

♦ "I thought I would be the great American writer by thirty years old, then at thirty-four Seth appeared."

♦ "When I was writing *Aspect Psychology* (Part Two of *Adventures in Consciousness*) I worked from an intellectual point, yet my intellect worked as automatically as the body. Also, I was getting the book in my dreams every night."

♦ "It was funny to say I was 'working' on the book *Psychic Politics*, because it was more like 'getting it.'"

♦ "I wouldn't have class if I didn't get something out of it, or if you didn't get something out of it."

• "I don't mind being forty-six years old, but don't want to be forty-six and stupid." This comment by Jane was in response to a *Time Magazine* article in 1972 featuring Richard Bach, author of Jonathan Living Seagull, in which he described Jane as "a *middle-aged* woman in a rocking chair." (Richard Bach, by the way, visited with Jane numerous times and interacted with Seth on various occasions.)

• "As far as I am concerned, nobody has found any good answers."

• "The fact that I questioned Seth's material shocked people. The idea is to try it out, to test it out."

• "I do what I do in spite of my fear, or maybe, because of it."

• "The pyramid I sense with Seth II is also in some way composed of sound patterns."

• "Sometimes I was concerned about having Seth II come through because someone might get frightened."

• "I do myself for myself."

• "I always liked bars and thought they were great places to be spontaneous."

• "As I looked over the class transcripts I realized that everything had a very strong purpose in class."

• "I still resent it when new people come to class with the attitude—will Seth come through?"

• "When we make fun of Seth to show we are not putting him on a pedestal, we are making fun of portions of our own psyche."

+ "Each person can do things with his or her consciousness that nobody else can, because each person's consciousness is unlike anybody else's."

+ "I was so scared for the first year and a half I had classes, that I wouldn't let Seth come through."

+ "Sometimes I have to mentally say, 'Seth, enough for now.'"

+ "You can meet your elbow in a flower."

+ "What we learn or remember, in the remembering becomes something new."

+ "I just turn over this way and see what's happening there. Our consciousness can go safely in any direction."

+ "You can watch your beliefs go out and create your reality."

+ "Seth could talk to me till I was blue in the face. I could say 'I see,' but sometimes it just wouldn't hit."

+ "When you think this stuff is something different, outside of the natural order, you're in trouble."

+ "The minus sign of sound turns into a different kind of plus that can direct matter. As everybody speaks, sound has a shape. The shape of sound is related to echo, and you can step into your own sound shape. Sounds move molecules and thus have a shape. Think in terms of inside sound and outside sound. Walk from the outside sound of my voice to the inside sounds within you, and it will have a color and a shape, even the inside of your eye, or any organ. Music that gives your body your life, inner sound of atoms, an ever-changing symphony."

+ "Silence within sound is the non-event. Beyond sound is not silence, but sounds on the other side of sound. Sometimes I experience sound in a very intense way."

+ "I've translated long sounds into the Seth voice. You are also translating your self through sounds from one frame of reference to physical reality."

+ "Don't forget, you create the great things in your reality too."

+ "Never try to escape your life or want someone else's life, or want to exchange your troubles with theirs. The problems are challenges and the answers are within them."

+ "An event in time is like an object in space; like a kid looking at a table and only able to see a part of it."

+ "There are emotional realities I have left aside to do what I do."

+ "I hate typing my material and I'm a lousy speller."

+ "Reincarnation made no sense to me for many years and I am still working things through."

+ "My awareness of Rob's Nebene aspect allowed me to deal with Rob better when that aspect showed itself." (For more about "Nebene," see Chapter Five in Jane's book, *Adventures in Consciousness*.)

+ "Sometimes I get Sumari and the English translation at the same time."

+ "When I sing Sumari I get it as colored sound."

◆   "Sumari pinpoints conflicts that block energy and helps solve them, and this helps heal the body. Sumari songs affect particular areas of the body."

◆   "Sumari in a certain way originates with you as well as with me. When you hear the sound, listen to your own body's reaction; that is, listen to yourselves as well as to what you hear from me, from Sumari."

◆   "I still need my own experiences as Jane, or I don't give a goddamn what anybody says. I started from scratch, and to free my intuitions even more I had to check out what I could do. People think I was born with all these goodies."

Our Parents Do Not Betray Us

An Unpublished Piece by Jane

During a class on July 23, 1974, Danny Stimmerman, a talented musician and songwriter, played some of the songs he had composed on his dulcimer. When he had finished, Jane asked him to continue playing.

As he played the dulcimer lightly in the background, Jane recited the following poem, creating it on the spot, without any pauses or hesitations. The effect was hypnotic, and I felt like I was witnessing creativity at the highest levels. Unfortunately, there is no tape of this, but at least we have a copy of the poem. I've entitled it, *Our Parents do not Betray Us*.

Our parents do not betray us,
Our parents do not betray us,
Our parents lead us into truth,
Our parents lead us sometimes unknowingly,
into roads and onto continents
that they may not understand,
But our parents do not betray us

They lead us and we lead ourselves into truth,
And so we do not lead our children into untruth,
nor do we betray them,
Nor need we fear the direction in which we lead our children,
For we lead our children into truth,
and all roads lead into truth

And when we think we are most forsaken,
and when we are the loneliest,
and when we cry out the loudest in our anguish,
then are we leading ourselves into truth.
There is no insect that does not know a portion of the truth,

There is no corner of a rock that does not stand up within
itself and shout,
and know a portion of the truth,
There is no angle or curve of a nerve or a neuron
or an ant
or a rock
or a plant,

That does not know its corner in the universe,
That does not stand up within itself and shout,
I am an event in the universe,
I am a portion of the truth,
and I am never betrayed into untruth

I stand up within myself and shout the nature of my being
and because I am, I am true
and there is no untruth

My parents did not lead me into untruth,
I do not fear that the earth will lead me into that which is
not, or to untruth,

For there is no flower that is untruth,
There is no spider or bug that is untruth,
There is no atom or molecule within my being that is
untruth,

Therefore each of us speak the truths that joyfully know
their being within us,
and we fear neither parent or children
And we follow with joy the direction in which our own
creativity and being spring

Part Two

The dawn comes without my knowing
The dawn comes, the day goes
The evening comes without my attention
the day is given to me
The earth grows about me and all is given

I come unknowing upon the face of the earth
yet all is provided,
The fruits of the earth grow about me,
The seasons come and go,
I can sit and think, yet my thinking while important to
me
seems at least not to affect the seasons
They come even when I do not believe in it
The apples grow in the trees even when I am despondent
The dawn comes,
even when it seems to me that there will never be another
dawn

The rains fall,
when my soul is parched,
When it seems to me that there is no divine moisture in
the universe,
Still the rains fall, and the grasses grow,
And my body grows,
even while I wonder what my body is

And some wisdom within me is as wise as an oak tree,
The oak tree grows, and I grow,
And when I learn consciously to grow in that same
knowledge,
Then I can speak to the oak tree,

and understand what the oak tree knows,
And then also I can teach the oak tree,
And I can say,
I know where your acorns come from,
they come from where my thoughts come from,
And if I follow my thoughts,
I will find where your oak comes from,
where your roots come from,

And if we follow our dreams,
we may awaken to find ourselves the flowers in another
universe,
or the rain that falls from other skies

How can I not trust my being
when the oak grows,
and the flower grows,
And the spider trusts its own reality in a corner of my
staircase,
How can I not be as daring as that spider,
How can I not trust my being
when the spider does.